HEALTHY THAI
COOKING

HEALTHY THAI COOKING

SRI OWEN

PHOTOGRAPHS BY JAMES MURPHY

SERIES EDITOR
LEWIS ESSON

STEWART, TABORI & CHANG
New York

For Roger

First published in 1997
by Frances Lincoln Limited
4 Torriano Mews
Torriano Avenue
London NW5 2RZ, England
Copyright © 1997
Frances Lincoln Limited

Text copyright © 1997 Sri Owen
Photographs copyright © 1997
James Murphy

Published in 1997 and distributed
in the U.S. by Stewart, Tabori & Chang,
a division of U.S. Media Holdings, Inc.
575 Broadway, New York, N.Y. 10012

Distributed in Canada by
General Publishing Co. Ltd.
30 Lesmill Road, Don Mills, Ontario, Canada M3B 2T6

Library of Congress Cataloging-in-Publication Data

Owen, Sri
    Healthy Thai Cooking / by Sri Owen: Photographs by
    James Murphy.
        p.   cm.
    ISBN 1 55670 539 5
    1. Cookery, Thai   I. Title
    TX724.5.T5083   1997
    641.59593–dc21   96-49512
                          CIP

Designed by Frances Lincoln Limited

Printed and bound in Hong Kong

10 9 8 7 6 5 4 3 2 1

CONTENTS

A FAMILIAR MYSTERY

All over the country, Thai food is a familiar mystery. Thai ingredients are increasingly available in Thai, Asian, and general gourmet markets, and Thai restaurants flourish and multiply. Yet when compared to other Asian cuisines, Thai cooking in the West has made very few concessions to Western tastes. The manners, the atmosphere, the attitude to food and eating, are all purely Thai, and so as a rule is the menu.

Whereas Chinese and Indian restaurants in Western cities long ago changed their ways and their recipes to appeal to the widest possible market, Thais, by and large, have not done this. They remain themselves, welcoming you to eat their food because they are confident you will enjoy it just the way they like it—perhaps with a little less chili. That is why Thai cooking, however familiar it seems, remains a challenge to so many people. Yet it need not, and this book is written in the belief that true enjoyment comes from knowledge and understanding. The best Thai food is always the food you cook yourself in your own home.

Are Thai people healthy? I think Asians, as long as they are not too poor or too rich, generally eat better—more sensibly—than Westerners. Indeed, the Thai diet—rice and noodles, vegetables, fish, a little meat, little or no alcohol—sounds like a prescription for the good life, and it is. The point is that in Thailand the good life is to be enjoyed, and food is to be enjoyed as the basis of it.

In Bangkok, shopping is nearly as much of a skill as cooking, and it is a social art as well. Every quarter of the city has its market, and these are wonderful places to explore, even for the tourist: generally clean, well-organized, accessible, and humming with life.

Everything has been brought in fresh that morning, and everything will be sold by late afternoon; only a few staples or preserves have long shelf lives. At one stall, a dozen varieties of rice are neatly labeled; at another, the pink or silver flanks of fish rise from beds of crushed ice. A woman weighs and packs vivid red and green chilies; her neighbor turns the handle of a machine that grates coconut flesh. A girl fans glowing charcoal beneath a huge wok of roasting peanuts, or offers you a newly fried spring roll. In smaller towns and villages, of course, markets are even more important to the community.

Reaching out from the marketplace, penetrating the city center and still numerous in the suburbs, street food vendors ply a vigorous trade in every part of Thailand, as they have always done. The visitor should approach street food with caution, but anything you see cooked in front of you is probably safe to eat, if sometimes a bit indigestible. It may, of course, be powerfully laced with chili. There are small restaurants everywhere, as one would expect. Local knowledge or friendly advice is needed if the short-stay visitor is to find the really good ones. If you can afford it, a four- or five-star hotel restaurant is often the best place to eat real Thai food, because the chef will be trained in presenting food the way foreigners like it. You will still have real Thai cooking and authentic flavors, but you will not have to cope with fish or chickens that seem to be all bones or curry that sears your palate.

The principles of healthy and good cooking are the same in Thailand as they are anywhere else. The ingredients should be nutritious; the cooking methods should preserve the goodness of these ingredients; and the selection of dishes should be such as to contribute to a well-balanced diet.

THAI TASTE

What does a typical Thai meal consist of and what is special about Thai food, from the point of view both of flavor and of nutrition?

Taking the second question first, my answer is that Thai cooking appeals to us through its aromatic freshness, and that the food in this book has the extra appeal of lightness. This doesn't mean that you can't overeat, and I have risen from many a Thai feast feeling distinctly full yet wishing I had room for more. However, the fullness comes largely from rice, which is the most all-around satisfying staple food on this planet. Rice is mainly starch, in a form easily digested and conveyed to the muscles over a period of about 24 hours after the meal as glycogen, ready to be converted into energy. It has no "bad" cholesterol, no gluten, and no tooth-decaying sugar. It has a few B-group vitamins, trace minerals, a little dietary fiber, and some proteins. The proteins combine with the proteins in soybean products, such as tofu, to give us good daily amounts of all the amino acids our bodies require; this is particularly useful for vegetarians.

Most Asians eat a lot of vegetables anyway, because meat is expensive. The sea provides a daily harvest of fish and shellfish; the rivers and flooded rice fields sustain more fish, eels, frogs, and ducks. Everyone keeps chickens, and perhaps a pig, because they eat household scraps. There are enough patches of rough grass to feed a few goats, but most of the fodder was needed, until recently, for the buffaloes that plowed the rice fields. Conditions are unsuitable for keeping cows; still less would anyone use precious land to grow crops simply for the fattening of beef. So there are no dairy products and very few heavy meat dishes. Instead, there are wonderful sharp-tasting salads, spicy seafood and soups, a vast range of what are conventionally called "curries" (because, like Indian curries, they are flavored with pastes containing mixtures of spices), vegetables lightly cooked to retain their natural textures and food values, and lots of fresh fruit. Much of this list reads like a doctor's prescription for a healthy diet.

Much, but not all. The traveler in Thailand will notice that typical menus contain a lot of fried food, some of it very oily. Much of the food is very sweet, and one of the tastes that Thais use to balance this sweetness is salt. Then there is the dreaded monosodium glutamate: I can say from experience that one of the hardest tasks in a kitchen is to persuade a Thai cook that MSG is not needed in anybody's food, except when it occurs naturally (as in soy sauce) and in very small amounts. The traditional Thai diet is certainly healthy, but it contains elements that we can remove in order to make it healthier still, without losing anything vital on the gastronomic side.

In the world league table of culinary excellence—a fantasy league if ever there was one—Thailand has been steadily improving its position as the reputation of its food spreads. One factor has been the number of non-Thai cooks who have fallen in love with Thai flavors and dashed home to experiment. Lemongrass, almost unobtainable in the West twenty years ago, is now widely available. Anyone who enjoys cooking and who becomes familiar with Thai cuisine will soon want to introduce these flavors into their own dishes.

In my experience, however, this "fusion" cuisine—to give it its currently fashionable name—can work well only if the cook is familiar with both the fused traditions. I abandoned long ago the idea that everything in cooking should be authentic, but I am still a purist in my belief that every ingredient should be of the best quality and that its character should be right for the use to which it is put.

For example, I will defend my use of olive oil in my own Thai cooking against anyone who insists that there is no olive oil in Thailand. Olive oil indeed is not "authentic," but it is healthy, and food cooked in it will taste good.

EATING IN THE THAI MANNER

Rice is the center of every meal in Thailand, as elsewhere in Southeast Asia. It is much more than a staple food; it is a cornerstone of Thai society and culture. If you fill yourself with other food, but have not eaten rice, then you have not really eaten at all.

A regular Thai meal consists of cooked rice, soup, curry, and condiments or side dishes, with several other dishes that are steamed, fried, or grilled. There will also be a strong hot dip with vegetables and fish. For a big family celebration, or to entertain guests, there may be a great many of these side dishes; at a small family supper in the city, where both parents have done a day's work, there may be only two or three. In either case, table manners are informal. Each person has a soup plate and a spoon and fork. The spoon is necessary, because some of the dishes are liquid, but a knife is not needed, because all the food has been cut up before cooking. You help yourself to a good large pile of rice and to one or two of the other dishes; when you have sampled these, move on to one or two others; and so work your way round the whole array, or as much of it as you want to, not waiting to be invited but paying the cook the compliment of eating plenty of what he or she has set before you. It is good manners to eat heartily and appreciatively, but not to overeat, or to pile your plate from every dish at once. The meal usually ends with two desserts, one dry and one with liquid, and some fruit.

All these elements can be rearranged to fit the Western pattern of three (or more) courses. However, I would suggest that anyone who is not yet familiar with this type of cooking should start by cooking and serving just one dish at a sitting. This pattern of a one-dish meal, whether the recipe is taken from the Snacks & Appetizers section, the soups, or one of the sections of main-course dishes, will lead you at once into a pattern of more healthy eating.

SOME NOTES ON NUTRITION

The figures given in the nutritional information panel that accompanies each recipe are per serving and have been rounded off to the nearest whole number. Optional ingredients and variations have not been included in the calculations and the figures are based on the largest number of suggested servings.

The percentage of the total calories in each dish contributed by fat is given in brackets after the total fat figure per serving. Please note that such a figure can occasionally produce results that seem surprising when not viewed in a wider context. For example, a relish made with only 2 tablespoons of oil can have a very low overall calorie count, so its fat content then reads as a fairly high percentage. However, were that relish to be analyzed together with an accompanying bowl of rice, the increase in total calories could reduce the level of fat to a medium, or even low, percentage.

As the fats in coconut can be as much as 98% saturated, throughout this book the coconut milk and cream content of dishes have been reduced from traditional generous levels. If you are attempting to curb saturated fat intake, you may lower them further. However, their use has been kept at an optimum level to achieve authentic flavors.

Many Thai dishes make generous use of seafood and seafood products, so cholesterol levels can appear high. Bear in mind, however, that the healthy metabolism self-regulates blood cholesterol levels if it is not subverted by a diet also high in saturated fats. Also, cholesterol itself is made up of both harmful and beneficial elements: "bad" cholesterol contains a high proportion of low-density lipoproteins (LDLs), which cause blood cholesterol to be deposited on the arterial walls and, "good" cholesterol is rich in high-density lipoproteins (HDLs) which work against the activity of the LDLs and themselves help lower blood cholesterol levels.

SOME THAI INGREDIENTS

All the recipes in this book have been tested using ingredients bought in London. Most are available from a good American supermarket. More exotic items can be found in speciality food stores: gourmet and health food stores and Thai, Indian, Chinese, and Japanese food stores. (A good Chinese market carries almost everything.) Wherever possible, I have tried to suggest substitutes for any ingredient that may be a real problem.

FRUIT

DURIAN

This is a famous love-it-or-loathe-it tropical fruit, so strong-smelling that it is banned from public transport and hotels even in durian-mad places like Bangkok, where almost everyone is a durian addict. Fresh durians are now exported from Thailand when in season, but they cost the earth, and you are also paying for the thick greenish-brown skin studded with sharp spikes. You can however quite often buy packaged frozen—and skinless—pale yellow durian chunks in Thai or Chinese stores. These are excellent for ice cream.

JACKFRUIT

When in season, fresh jackfruit can be found in Asian shops, but they are often very large and you may not want to tackle a whole one. They also contain a sticky juice that is difficult to remove from skin and clothing. Ripe ones, which are yellowish-brown on the outside with orange-colored flesh, are eaten as fruit, not cooked. For cooking, buy green (unripe) jackfruit in cans.

MANGO

Mangoes need no introduction and everyone loves them. When buying mangoes, avoid ones that are overripe and soft; green (unripe) mangoes are specified for several non-dessert recipes in this book. Mangoes are rich in vitamins A, B, and C; and green mangoes can contain up to 130 mg of vitamin C per 100 g. Unfortunately, they also have a high sugar content, up to 20 percent of their weight.

To get the flesh from a mango: peel it, then cut the flesh from the pit in thick slices or chunks. Alternatively, cut off large unpeeled pieces from around the pit. Score the flesh in ½-inch squares, and then press the skin up to separate the squares of flesh.

PAPAYA

The Spanish introduced papayas, or papaws, to the East from Central America, and they are now grown everywhere. Ripe Thai papayas are considered to be the sweetest. For the Thais, and most other Asians, green (unripe) papayas are both vegetable and fruit, often cooked with meat or fish, and used in salads like the Green Papaya and Carrot Salad on page 56. The fruit contains papain, an enzyme which helps to tenderize meat and has many medicinal properties—it is a diuretic and aids digestion.

PINEAPPLE

I find it very difficult to choose a perfect pineapple. From the·outside, it can look good, it can have the right color and smell, the right shape, everything. However, because they are so delicate and easily bruised, pineapples are usually imported when they are still green, then ripened in storage. They ripen slowly, and you need luck as well as judgment to get one that is perfectly ripe at the moment you need it.

Pineapple is a good source of vitamin C and, like papaya, has a high content of the enzyme papain. I do not recommend replacing fresh pineapple with canned.

POMELO

This citrus fruit, considerably larger than a grapefruit, is a native of Thailand, Indonesia, and Malaysia. Thailand exports more pomelos than the other two countries, so everything you buy from a Thai store will be the Thai variety. Pomelos are also grown now in Israel, and this is what you usually get in supermarkets.

The rind is very thick, green or yellowish in color. It can be candied and made into marmalade. The firm flesh is pale yellow, cream, or pink, and much less juicy than the grapefruit's. Some varieties are very sweet, without any trace of bitterness; some are more refreshing, with a little sourness. There is no indication at all from the outside of either the taste or the color of the flesh. Just try to choose a firm round one without any blemishes on the rind.

To open a pomelo, you need to cut the thick rind from both ends of the fruit with a sharp knife, and score deeply around the remaining rind in several places so that you can pull it off in strips. Now you have a round fruit with a thick white pith; you can peel this off with a sharp knife until you get to the membranes that hold the segments of the fruit. When you tear these away you will see that the flesh is contained in long sacs, which can be broken off in largish clusters. They are used in several salad recipes in this book. Naturally, they can also be used in a fruit salad, or simply eaten by themselves.

VEGETABLES

BEAN SPROUTS

The sprouts sold in plastic packets at most greengrocers, supermarkets, and Asian food shops are nearly always those of mung beans. Ideally, the brown root should be torn off each sprout and discarded and the sprouts washed in cold water; this is a tedious job, but it does improve the appearance of the dish. A few years ago, bean sprouts were considered extremely nutritious. Today they are less highly regarded, though they are rich in Vitamin C and contain some iron and B vitamins. They are, however, mostly water, and I am sceptical about claims made for them as a health food. On the other hand, their appearance, taste, and crispness make them well worth having.

EGGPLANTS

Eggplants are members of the genus *Solanum*, which includes potatoes, tomatoes, peppers, tobacco, and deadly nightshade. They are not limited to the shiny purple zeppelins that for years were the only variety widely available in the U.S. Round white eggplants, a bit bigger than a golf ball, can now sometimes be found but the most common eggplant that will suit the recipes in this book is the so-called Japanese or Chinese eggplant that is around 2 inches wide and 10 inches long. Pea eggplants—not much bigger than large green peas, and usually sold on the stem—can sometimes be found in Thai stores. When cooked, they are still quite hard and have an agreeably bitter taste.

LENTILS

Lentils (labeled *dhal* in Indian stores) have been cultivated longer than any other legume—probably for some 9,000 years. They are pulses—seeds growing in pods—and are dried so that they keep long in storage. Unlike most legumes, however, they do not need to be soaked before use. All legumes are rich in proteins, iron, and B vitamins; the amino acids of their proteins complement those of rice, so a lentil-and-rice based diet is nourishing and relatively cheap. I use red lentils or split mung beans in the sauce recipe for Vegetarian Rice Noodles on page 105.

Water Spinach

Also known as Chinese water spinach or "swamp cabbage" this vegetable is in fact grown in many other countries: Thailand, of course, Malaysia and Indonesia among others. It has soft green leaves that resemble spinach, but the stems are hollow. You need to discard about 2 inches of the tough stalk. The rest must be cleaned thoroughly by cutting the hollow stems lengthwise, so that no mud stays inside. This plant has a high water content and does not keep well. Buy only the leaves that still look fresh and unwilted, and use within 24 hours.

Yard-long Beans

Also called snake beans, these are green beans that can actually grow up to a yard long. Snap one with your fingers; if it snaps easily, it is fresh. If you need to cut them with a knife, the beans are old and fibrous. If you can't find yard-long beans, use ordinary young green beans.

COCONUT AND COCONUT PRODUCTS

Coconut is said to be one of the world's most universally popular flavors and plays a leading part in most tropical cooking because it is so versatile. Coconut milk is used all over Southeast Asia as a cooking medium. This is not the sweet liquid that pours out of the nut when you break it; that is coconut water. The milk is extracted from the white flesh by grating and pressing. You can buy coconut milk in cans, but you will get better results if you make your own, starting either from a whole nut or from a package of desiccated (dried, unsweetened) coconut.

If you live in a coconut-producing area you will be familiar with coconuts of various ages and types. If not,

then the only coconut you need to know about is the one you buy in the local market—brown, hard-shelled, and covered in coarse fiber. When you choose one, give it a shake; you should hear the water slopping about inside.

To open a mature coconut, start by giving its shell a number of sharp taps with a hammer or the back of a cleaver. This will loosen the flesh, and the shell may eventually start to crack. Put the nut inside a plastic bag if you don't want the sweet, sticky water all over the floor. Give the shell a few harder blows; it will soon give way. Usually, the flesh splits open with the shell and sticks to it, but sometimes the flesh remains intact, which saves you the trouble of prising it away from the fragments of shell. The coconut water is frankly not worth saving, and is always full of bits of fiber and shell, but if you like very sweet water you can strain and drink it.

Coconut flesh comes from the shell with a thin brown skin. For light-colored dishes, particularly sweets, this must be peeled off and discarded, but for the pressing of coconut milk the skin can be left on.

Nutritionally, the coconut is problematic. Coconut oil, because it is the non-animal fat with the highest proportion of saturates, is often viewed with suspicion. This is somewhat unjustified because, as well as being totally without cholesterol (unlike similarly saturated animal fats), it is one of the best sources of medium-chain fats. These are thought to play a very important role in the metabolizing of fats in general. Indeed many coconut-based drugs make use of this property. The coconut is also very rich in iron.

Throughout the recipes in this book I have, of course, tried to reduce the large quantities of coconut milk traditional in many Thai dishes to keep calories and saturated fat levels low. However, its use is often essential for both flavor and texture—and I am also certain that in moderate amounts it is not harmful.

Desiccated (Dried, Unsweetened) Coconut

If you buy this in small packages with a sell-by date, you will get good stuff, but it will be rather expensive. You need quite a lot to make coconut milk, so buy 1-pound or 2-pound bags from an Asian market or a health food store. There is often no sell-by date, so sniff the bag: rancid coconut is easily detectable.

Coconut Milk

To make about 2½ cups of "thick" or "first extraction" milk you will need the grated flesh of 1 fresh coconut, or 12 ounces desiccated coconut and 2½ cups of hot water. To make it by hand: pour the water over the coconut (simmer desiccated coconut for 4 to 5 minutes first) and let it cool until you can put your hand into it comfortably. Squeeze handfuls of flesh well to press the liquid out, and strain through a fine sieve. To make it in a blender: put the coconut and half the water into the blender and blend for 20 to 30 seconds. Squeeze and sieve as above. Put the coconut back in the blender with the rest of the water, and repeat.

Coconut milk can be stored in an airtight container in the refrigerator for up to 48 hours. An opaque white "cream" rises to the top, where it may become solid. The two parts can simply be stirred together again. Coconut milk does not freeze well. If cooking for the freezer, omit the coconut milk until you thaw the dish ready to reheat.

Creamed Coconut

Coconut oils and other fats are factory-processed to produce this substance, which is sold in a hard white block. It is not the same as the coconut cream which forms on top of the milk as described above, and it is not a substitute for coconut milk; it cannot be used as a cooking medium from the start of cooking. It is useful, however, when added to a dish at the end of cooking, either to thicken the sauce or to give extra coconut flavor.

RICE, NOODLES, AND MISCELLANEA

Rice

This is not only the most satisfying and tasty of all staple foods, it is also one of the most nutritious. Its starches are easily converted by the body to glycogen, which fuels the muscles. White rice provides a limited but useful range of B group vitamins and some protein—the amino acids of which complement those in soya beans and lentils. It also contains small amounts of phosphorus, zinc, selenium, copper, and iodine, and provides dietary fiber. It contains no salt, gluten, or extrinsic sugars (those that rot teeth).

Unpolished brown rice is healthier still, because its bran coat is rich in vitamins and oils. However, no self-respecting Thai eats unpolished rice, and the loss of bran is amply compensated by the rest of their diet. Every Thai is a rice gourmet and eats only the best that he can afford.

More about rice will be found in the introduction to the section on Rice & Noodles (page 98).

Rice Powder

This is rice flour ground extra fine. If the recipe specifies powder, then rice flour is likely to be too coarse.

Cellophane Vermicelli

Also called glass or bean thread vermicelli or bean thread noodles, these are very thin, translucent noodles made from mung beans, looking like skeins of white wires.

Rice Noodles

The rice noodles commonly used by the Thais are thin vermicelli made from rice flour. They are as fine as the cellophane vermicelli above, but opaque. There are other types of rice noodles, notably the flat, ribbonlike ones, varying in width from about ¼ inch to 1¼ inches. Also called rice sticks, they are commonly used in Vietnamese and Chinese or Singaporean noodle dishes.

Spring Roll Wrappers

These are thin pastry squares that are essential for making spring rolls. They can be bought, usually frozen, and come in several sizes. I use 5-inch squares for the Miniature Spring Rolls on page 32. For bigger spring rolls, buy the 8½-inch squares.

The pastry gets dry very easily, so the best way to work with it is to thaw the whole package completely and then peel the sheets off carefully, one by one; you can then freeze again the ones you don't need immediately. Once they have been separated, they stay separated, and you can fill and roll them quickly, even after they have been refrozen. Refreezing the wrappers is perfectly safe, as they are only made from flour and water.

Wonton Skins

These are sold fresh in packages or by weight; they are just 3-inch squares of very thin pastry. Wonton skins are also readily available frozen. This pastry is made with eggs, so the squares don't stick to each other as the spring roll wrappers do.

Tofu

This is a soft, creamy substance made from the liquid pressed out of cooked soya beans, the most protein-rich of the legumes. It is also called bean curd, but the Japanese word *tofu* is nowadays probably better known. Tofu contains much of the nutritional value of soya beans, including the proteins. Firm Chinese-style tofu is best cooked before it is eaten; the plain tofu is bland and rather textureless, but it makes an excellent foundation for many savory dishes (and some sweets). It can be bought fresh in most supermarkets and health food stores and kept in the refrigerator: brand-name tofu is usually stamped with a use-by date.

Asian shops sell blocks of firm Chinese-style tofu characteristically packaged in water, sealed in plastic containers. This type of tofu cannot be kept any longer than about five days, and after the first day or two the water should be changed daily. Tofu that has gone bad has an unpleasant smell, and it is unlikely that anyone would propose to eat it.

Japanese manufacturers also export "silken" tofu in sealed cartons, which can keep unopened for a long time. It is, however, very soft, and is not always suitable for recipes in this book, except for soups and the Scrambled Tofu and Eggs on page 138. Silken tofu is often used uncooked, blended as a base for sauces, dressings, and sweet dishes in place of yogurt or cream.

I usually specify Chinese-style tofu in my recipes because it cooks better and has more flavor. If you can't get the Chinese type, buy Japanese "cotton" tofu, which is packed in a similar way to the silken but is firmer. You can also buy pre-fried firm tofu, which is dark-brown in color.

AGAR-AGAR

This extract from a kind of tropical seaweed gels at room temperature and thus makes an excellent vegetarian substitute for gelatin. Packets of whitish strands or granules may be bought at most Asian markets. Don't use more than the recipe suggests—too much produces an unpleasantly rubbery texture.

OILS

PEANUT OIL

The peanut is, strictly speaking, a legume, not a nut. Unlike most legumes, peanuts and soybeans store energy for the young seedling as oil, not as starch. Peanut oil is excellent for frying, as it does not affect the flavor of the food and takes the high temperatures of stir-frying well. Like most other vegetable oils, it is also low in saturates.

OLIVE OIL

The olive is unknown in Thailand, since it will not grow under tropical conditions; but Thai cooks are beginning to discover imported olive oil, and I make no apology for using it in some recipes, since it is so good in itself and, of course, good for you—indeed it is seen as a key element in the "healthiness" of the Mediterranean diet. The monounsaturates of which it has a high proportion contain elements that both lower blood cholesterol and act against the very agents that cause cholesterol to be deposited as plaque on arterial walls. It is also rich in vitamin E.

AROMATIC FLAVORINGS

ASIAN CELERY

This is perhaps better known as Chinese celery; the Chinese name is *heung kun*. It has thin stalks and abundant delicately flavored leaves, greener than those of Western celery, and it is these that are used in cooking. If you cannot find Asian celery, the inner young stalks and leaves of ordinary celery make an adequate substitute.

BASIL

Thailand produces several varieties of basil, at least two of which are exported. *Horapha* or *manglak* has large, light green leaves, tastes of aniseed, and is very similar to Western "sweet" basil; it is available almost anywhere. The other has narrower, darker leaves and purplish stems, and is difficult to find except in Thai shops. The Thai name for this is *kaprow* or *kaprow pa*.

CORIANDER (CILANTRO)

This is a very important flavoring and garnish in Thailand, where the leaves, seeds, and roots are all used. Leaves and seeds are easily bought almost anywhere. Roots are harder to find, because they are usually cut off before they reach the greengrocer; buy all you come across and freeze them. The root is the only part that can be frozen. Fresh green coriander is also known as cilantro.

MIANG LEAVES

These large, dark green, oval or heart-shaped leaves can be bought from Thai shops that receive fresh produce from Thailand by air. They are used as edible uncooked wrappers. Miang in fact means "snack," or has come to refer to snacks, but there seem to be several other Thai names for the leaf. As far as I can discover, its botanical name is *Piper sarmentosum*, sometimes called in English wild betel leaf.

SHALLOTS

I use shallots where the Thais would use their very small red onions; these onions are sometimes obtainable in Thai stores, but shallots, particularly the red-tinged variety, make a good substitute.

TURMERIC

This spice, related to ginger, has a warm, rich aroma, but it is also used because it gives a dish, particularly a rice dish, a golden yellow color—the color, in Asia, of royalty and celebration. Indeed, turmeric is much used as a dye.

Fresh turmeric roots are often available. The best flavor is said to be in the short stubby "fingers" which grow off the main root. You peel the root as if you were peeling ginger, then put it in the blender to make a paste. Be careful not to get the juice on your clothes, because it won't wash off. If using ground dried turmeric, look for a good deep color and strong aroma.

Like many spices, turmeric is carminative and helps to dispel gas. It is also a potent antiseptic and in many parts of the world is used in ointments to treat wounds and skin diseases.

HOT FLAVORINGS

CHILIES

In this book we are concerned only with four or five types of chili that are easily available. In countries where chilies are grown, particularly in Central America and the U.S., you will find a much wider selection. If you cannot find fresh chilies, dried chilies are good for most cooked dishes. Chili powder is all right as a flavoring if you can't find whole chilies, but it goes stale very quickly and tends only to have heat and not much flavor.

Most chilies start out green and then turn red as they ripen. Choice of color depends largely on how well it will match or contrast with the color of the food it is to go with. Unripe and ripe chilies taste more or less equally hot: the hotness comes from a compound called capsaicin, which is concentrated in the membrane to which the seeds are attached. If you remove the seeds, most of the membrane comes away with them, and you are left with the outer fruit wall and the skin, which have the pungent, distinctive flavor of the chili but very little of its fiery hotness.

Some of the chilies shown in the picture opposite are as follows. The wide, blunt-nosed chili, 1½ to 2 inches long, with smooth, shiny skin, sold and used while still green, is mildly hot. The long green and long red chili, used in most of the recipes in this book, 3 to 4 inches long, narrow, sharply pointed, often curved, is hot. The medium green or red chili, 1 to 1½ inches long, narrow and pointed, with smooth skin, is very hot. The tiny red or green "bird chili," about 1 inch long, is extremely hot. (For the record, the hottest of all chilies is the habanero or Scotch bonnet.)

The human mouth, fingertip, skin in general, and eyes, can all detect capsaicin in infinitesimally small amounts. Therefore, handle all fresh and dried chilies with care. Many cooks wear rubber gloves, but you can prevent any burning sensation by rubbing your hands with plenty of salt or vegetable oil before touching chilies. When you have finished, wash your hands well. Don't rub or touch your eyes, or any other sensitive area, with fingers that have just touched a chili.

Despite its apparent fierceness, capsaicin is actually harmless; it does not burn or inflame any part of the body for more than a minute or two, and does not cause cancer unless ingested in impossibly huge quantities. (It is actually said to protect against some cancers.) If you get it in your eye, it will sting painfully but will not have any lasting effect. If you get a very hot mouthful of chili, the pain will not last; you can relieve it by drinking iced water or eating some cold boiled rice, but a glass of cold milk is even more effective.

All chilies are rich in vitamins A and C and many other nutrients; this includes dried chilies and chili flakes, in which they are even more concentrated.

Chili Oil

This is oil that has been flavored and preserved with chilies. Ready-made chili oils are now widely available in good food stores and some supermarkets, or you can make your own by steeping chilies for several weeks in peanut, sesame, or corn oil and then straining it. Chili oil is used in salad dressings or in dishes needing only a slight hint of chili flavor.

GINGER

Fresh ginger can be bought almost everywhere: when you buy it, it should feel firm and look smooth and clear-skinned. Buy a little at a time, so that it does not go stale in storage. In fact, ginger freezes very well and can be grated from frozen with great ease.

For most dishes, ginger is peeled and then it is either chopped, sliced thinly, or put in the blender along with other ingredients for a paste. Vary the amount of ginger to suit your own taste. If you only want a subtle hint of it to flavor the food, cut it into two or three large pieces that can then be found and removed before the dish is served. Dried and pickled ginger are also good for cooking, but avoid the powdered variety which loses what little flavor it has very rapidly.

Ginger helps the digestion by reducing flatulence and promoting that pleasant feeling of relaxed well-being that the stomach expects after a good meal. It is also said to stimulate the circulation and some people use it as an antidote to travel sickness.

Ginger Juice

This is recommended for a few delicate dishes in this book and for those who only like the mildest hint of ginger. To make ginger juice: peel a good-sized piece of ginger and put it into a blender with 1 tablespoon of warm water, then pass it through a fine sieve. It may then be frozen in ice cube trays. Small amounts of ginger juice can be obtained quickly by crushing chunks in a garlic press. A mixture of ginger juice and lime or lemon juice in hot water is a traditional Thai remedy for colds and chills.

MOOLI

This is also known by its Japanese name of daikon, or simply white radish, which is an exact description. It is, however, very large, often 12 to 16 inches long. The flavor, similar to that of a Western radish but milder, is as popular in Indian cuisine as it is in those of the Far East. The mooli has diuretic properties and also aids the digestion.

PEPPER

In the shops, whole peppercorns are usually either black (that is, dark brown; the ripe berries are sun-dried and the skins left on) or white (the skins are removed, revealing the light brown flesh). Both black and white peppers are sold ready-ground, but ground pepper loses its flavor fairly quickly, so a pepper mill is useful in the kitchen as well as on the dining table. White pepper is useful for dishes, like pale sauces, the appearance of which may be marred by speckling.

Fresh green peppercorns are becoming popular in the West, and are what Thais themselves prefer to cook with. The berries are still on the stalk and should be bright green; they will stay fresh for a few days in the refrigerator. Because they have been picked before they are fully mature, they then soften and turn black and lose most of their hotness.

Green peppercorns can also be bought in bottles, pickled or preserved in brine. These are very aromatic and are currently quite fashionable.

SALTY FLAVORINGS

Salt itself is little used as a condiment in Asian cooking, as there are so many delicious flavorings that contribute saltiness. The main advantage of using seasonings like fish sauce and miso is that because of their powerful flavors less is needed and so sodium levels are kept low. Also, items like soy sauce are natural sources of monosodium glutamate, which enhances other flavors around it.

BLACK AND YELLOW BEANS; YELLOW BEAN SAUCE

Salted yellow beans, sold in cans or jars, are fermented soybeans. They need to be crushed to make a smooth paste. The label may say "Yellow Bean Sauce," in which case the beans are already crushed. Salted black beans, or "black bean sauce," are the same, but made from black soybeans.

FISH SAUCE

The Romans flavored their cooking with *garum*, a mixture of salt and well-rotted fish. Southeast Asian cooks do the same today, each region having its own favorite pungent paste or liquid. The Thais use it in liquid form and call it *nam pla*. You can buy large bottles of it quite cheaply at almost any Asian food store. Being diluted, it doesn't smell as strongly as shrimp paste and you are less likely to use too much. However, it is still salty and highly flavored, so don't use more than the recipe specifies.

MISO

This is a Japanese preparation of salted and fermented soybeans mixed into a paste with rice or barley. It is usually easy to find, in health food stores if nowhere else.

SHRIMP PASTE

This is used in southern Thailand, where the cooking has much in common with that of Malaysia and neighboring Indonesia. You can buy it in many Asian food stores, in hard blocks labeled *terasi, trassie, blachen,* or *balachan.* It must be dry-fried or roasted before use. The Thai shrimp paste is called *kapi,* and is usually available in small or large plastic or glass jars. The difference between *kapi* and *balachan* or *terasi* is that *kapi* is quite soft, so you can spoon it out of the jar. It will keep almost indefinitely if you store it in a well-secured airtight jar in a dry place, and you don't really need to refrigerate it. The smell of shrimp paste is powerful and the taste very strong—but the effect of even a small amount in a cooked dish is striking.

Dried Shrimp

The Thais make much use in their cooking of tiny shrimp that have been cooked and dried. They are sold in plastic packages at most Asian food stores in the West. In Malaysia and Indonesia they are called *ebi,* and in Thai they are *kung eang.* They are not very nice to eat by themselves, but add flavor and a slight chewy texture to dishes.

Soy Sauce

This is another of the range of salted, fermented soybean products developed over millennia in Southeast Asia. It is not Thai, but is widely used in Thailand in Chinese-style dishes. There is an essential distinction between light soy and dark soy sauce, light being saltier and dark sweeter (though still pretty salty). Chinese soy sauces are easily obtainable; so is the Japanese brand leader, Kikkoman, which is really a dark soy but can be used in any recipe that calls for soy sauce. Japanese soy sauces, also called *shoyu* or *tamari,* are healthy in that they are generally free of additives, including added sugar.

SOUR FLAVORINGS

Galingale or Galangal

This is a rhizome, looking rather like ginger but larger and pinker. The two plants are, however, unrelated and the taste of galingale—aromatic and slightly bitter—is completely different from that of ginger. Fresh galingale is now available in most Asian food stores (the Thai name is *ka* or *khaa*). It should be peeled and chopped, like ginger. Powdered galingale is generally available and will do well enough if you can't find fresh. Dried slices can also be bought; soak these in cold water just before use and discard before the dish is served. Never put a slice of dried galingale in your blender, however, as it is so hard that it will break the blender knife. Galingale contains an oil that is said to sweeten the breath and clear the respiratory passages as well as aiding the digestion.

Kaffir Lime

This small, green, pear-shaped, knobby-skinned citrus fruit is called *makrut* in Thailand. Its leaves and rind are used to give the lemony sourness that Southeast Asians love. It can be bought fresh in most Asian food stores. The dried rind (*piu makrut*), already cut in thin strips, is also imported; this should be soaked in warm water before use. A kaffir lime has very little juice in it, so when a recipe specifies lime juice, this is always the juice from an ordinary smooth-skinned lime.

Lemongrass

Nowadays, lemongrass hardly needs any introduction; it is the ingredient that comes first to most Westerners' minds when they think of Thai cooking. It looks like a coarse, heavy type of grass, and is used in many recipes for its sour-sweet citrus flavour. For most dishes, cut the stem into three pieces and wash; one of these pieces is usually sufficient. Remember to remove it before serving.

For curries, soups, and salad dressings, the outer leaves are stripped off (they can still be used in cooking, as above); only the tender inner part is used, chopped into rounds like a scallion and blended into a curry paste. For

soup and salad dressing, you just use these thin tiny slices raw. The lemongrass stalk can also be used as a skewer for fish satay (see page 68) or as a brush for painting marinade on satays or other meat or fish while grilling.

To make a brush, cut off and discard about ½ inch from the root end and beat the cut end of the stem, not too hard, with the handle of a knife or a meat pounder until you get a flexible lemongrass brush.

TAMARIND

This is the fruit of a tree that came originally from India. The seeds grow in pods: in each pod, several large, hard seeds are enclosed in the sour-tasting flesh. Tamarind can be bought in this form in many Asian stores, and this fresh ripe tamarind is the best kind to buy and use, because it has not been processed and mixed with artificial preservatives.

Tamarind Water

Tamarind can be made into tamarind water from the pulp you buy in blocks of 1 pound or in smaller packets. To make some tamarind water, which is called for in many recipes, break off a lump of pulp about as big as a walnut, soak it for a few minutes in about 6 tablespoons of warm water, and then press and squeeze it to drive out the brown juice into the water. Strain the resulting liquid, and discard the solids. Tamarind water does not look very attractive, but imparts a characteristic sourness to any dish.

If you use tamarind water often, it is worth making a small stock of it. Soak the whole 1-pound block of tamarind pulp in 5 cups of water in a saucepan for a few minutes. Then boil it for 3 minutes, and simmer for about a further 15 minutes. Pass the liquid through a sieve into another saucepan, and simmer for another 10 minutes to purify it further. Leave the liquid to get cold. It can now be stored in the refrigerator for up to 2 weeks, or can be frozen in an ice-cube tray and the cubes kept in the freezer for up to 3 months. One cube of frozen tamarind water is the equivalent of 1 tablespoon of tamarind water.

PICKLED GARLIC

Garlic has a reputation everywhere as a food that will cure practically every ailment and regular consumption of which almost guarantees a long healthy and vigorous life—it is antibacterial, anti-inflammatory, antioxidant, and helps lower blood cholesterol. I certainly can't imagine cooking without it, so as far as I am concerned its health-giving properties are just a bonus.

The Thais pickle the heavenly scented bulbs, and you can buy pickled garlic in any Thai or good Asian shop. It has a distinctive flavor that is quite different from that of fresh garlic. You can easily make your own pickled garlic—the recipe is on page 147.

RICE VINEGAR

Authentic original Japanese-style rice vinegar is made only from rice, water, and *koji*—a mold grown on cooked beans or grains. The finest rice vinegar can be produced only by traditional methods, involving much labor over a period of about one year. It is therefore expensive, even in Japan. It is, however, well worth getting and using good-quality rice vinegar. Its high acetic acid content counteracts lactic acid in the blood, reducing fatigue and protecting the joints against arteriosclerosis.

Japanese and Chinese food stores in the West sell a range of rice vinegars: Mitsukan is a typical good-quality brand and is reasonably priced. Check the list of ingredients—the vinegar should be prepared from alcohol and a natural grain extract made from wheat, *saké* cake (i.e., rice from which *sake* has been made), rice, and corn.

SWEET FLAVORINGS

CAPSICUMS

Sweet bell peppers are the mild cousins of the chilies. They are popular in most countries. It is easy to find brilliant red, green, and yellow peppers, with waxy skins and little flavor; my choice would be peppers imported from a sunnier climate rather than hot-house varieties.

PALM SUGAR / DEMERARA SUGAR

Palm sugar can sometimes be found in specialty Asian food stores (where it may also be labeled "jaggery," an Indian term). It should be made from the juice of coconut palm flowers, and be a dark red-brown color, though I often see it in Asian shops looking rather pale. The solid blocks are extremely hard; you have to either grate it or knock a piece off with a hammer and dissolve it. Demerara sugar—a British variety increasingly available here—is a good substitute. And if demerara sugar is unavailable, you will be safe using brown granulated sugar.

CRUNCHY TEXTURES

BAMBOO SHOOTS

These are easily obtainable in food stores and supermarkets, usually in cans, in chunks or already sliced. Very young bamboo shoots, looking almost like white asparagus, are sometimes sold in glass jars.

CASHEW NUTS

Cashews grow in pairs beneath large, pear-shaped, reddish-pink fruits that can be eaten raw or made into a sort of jam. As these fruits don't travel well, you never see them outside the tropics. Cashew nuts are always pricey, but are cheaper if you buy them by the pound in Asian shops. They must be roasted or fried in very hot oil for a few minutes before being eaten, not only because this makes them taste better but because raw cashews contain a mild poison which cooking destroys. The nuts are about 18 percent protein and contain a good deal of oil.

PEANUTS

Peanuts are not really nuts but a kind of bean that develops, in pods, under the ground. They are very nutritious and full of protein. Buy raw peanuts and dry-roast them yourself.

WATER CHESTNUTS

Fresh water chestnuts are now available in the West, but canned ones are still much easier to find. Of course, they are not chestnuts at all, but corms of a grass that grows under water.

CHEWY TEXTURES

MUSHROOMS

Thais use fresh straw mushrooms, which, as far as I know, are still not available in the West. Thai restaurants use canned straw mushrooms. Because they are so readily available I often use fresh button mushrooms, or chestnut (or brown) mushrooms for their flavor, or oyster mushrooms for their texture.

Cèpes (porcini)

Fresh cèpes are very expensive, but as their flavor is powerful, a small amount is all you need. Dried cèpes have even more flavor; soak them in warm water for at least 20 minutes before use. The strained soaking water is excellent for stock.

Shiitake Mushrooms

Japanese or Chinese in origin, delicious fresh shiitakes are now cultivated in the West, but are still very expensive. Like cèpes, dried shiitakes have a strong flavor. The dried stalks become very hard and are only good for stock.

Wood Ear or Dried Black Mushrooms/Fungus

These are very light, so you only need ½ to 1 ounce for most recipes. When soaked in hot water, they expand and become soft for slicing, but retain their crunchy texture.

WINE TO ACCOMPANY THAI FOOD

Thai food can provide the wine drinker with some intriguing challenges. The sourness of lime and galingale, the heat of ginger and chili, the complex mix of exotic flavors generally, have all encouraged the belief that water, tea, or beer are the only possible drinks.

True, some flavors are implacable assassins of wine, pineapple being perhaps the most notorious. However, very few of the appetizer or main-course dishes in this book contain pineapple. For the rest, if you are ready to jettison your prejudices, find your spirit of adventure, and exercise a little careful thought, wines can be selected that will accompany a Thai meal very creditably.

The key is to choose wines that are light, bright, and refreshing. White wines tend to fit the bill best. The

complex of flavors in the dishes demands wines that are simple and clean-cut. This means that experimentation need not be expensive; in general it is the cheaper end of the market that will work better. Simple but well-made wines may even be flattered by the right food.

SWEETNESS HELPS

A touch of sweetness in the wine often helps the partnership along. It calms the palate and helps to prevent the heat of spices from accumulating. What's wanted is just a little residual sugar: off-dry or *demi-sec*, rather than overtly sweet. Cheerful, sweetish "blush" wines have their part to play here. Surely such light and delicate wines will be overwhelmed? No. Chili and pepper, in particular, accentuate the flavor in wines; far from being overwhelmed, the flavors in the wine will be enhanced by the liaison. "Jug" wines designed for sociable quaffing can come out of such a combination surprisingly well. Other wines of a sweet disposition that can rise to the occasion include Vouvray *demi-sec* and some of the *vendange tardive* (late harvest) wines of Alsace, which are rarely sweet and often only off-dry.

THE ACIDITY FACTOR

We do also need to take account of grape variety, and to go for grapes that make wines with naturally high levels of acidity. The Riesling, native to Germany and Alsace but increasingly grown with great success in California and Australia, fits this category, as does the Chenin Blanc of Vouvray. Among the Alsace *vendange tardive* wines, Riesling, of course, or Tokay-Pinot Gris are the best to seek.

Acidity is needed because so many Thai dishes use lime flavors, either from the fruit itself or from kaffir lime leaves. Acidity in food diminishes the perception of acidity in wine; if you partner a Thai meal with a wine low in acidity, the wine is likely to seem dull and flabby.

Fruit, Fruit, and More Fruit

For the wine lover to whom such sweetness is anathema, the best option is to turn to the ultra-ripe wines of Australia. Go for unoaked wines redolent of vibrant fruit. Oaked wines tend to lose their fruit in combination with Thai food and can seem bitter or cardboardy. The peachy, pineappley (yes!), tropical-fruit flavors of unoaked Chardonnay strike natural chords with many Thai dishes, as do the Pacific Rim Rieslings of California and Australian Rieslings. Choose wines with as low an alcohol content as possible (blockbuster Chardonnays of 14 percent or more alcohol are not uncommon); otherwise the wine tends to overheat on the palate in combination with hot spices.

Other dry wines that can work well include the deliciously fresh Rieslings of New Zealand, and ripe Viognier or unoaked Chardonnay from southern France. Cheaper (less serious) Chardonnays (again without oak), or wines blended with Colombard grapes from the California wine regions, should also do nicely.

Herb and Spice Overload

However, there are also white wine grape varieties that are generally best avoided. One such is the aromatic Sauvignon Blanc, or Fumé Blanc as it is also called. Whatever its origin—California, Australia, or its homeland in the Loire Valley—and notwithstanding its zingy, fruit-laden, freshly acidic profile, its herbaceous character often clashes unpleasantly with the flavors in Thai cooking.

Another grape variety to approach with caution is the wildly aromatic Gewürztraminer. Despite its reputation for being an ideal choice to accompany "Oriental" cuisine, it has a tendency to become overblown. On the face of it, its lychees-and-roses character ought to work well, but its wines tend to lack acidity. With food, they all too easily cloy. More restrained wines from Gewürztraminer grapes work better, but tend to be expensive.

Avoid the Robust, the Tough, and the Tannic

If the occasion or the drinker demands a red wine, choose one that is light and easy. The last thing you want is anything remotely robust, tough, or tannic. A palate sensitized by spices doesn't need the rasping attack of tannins. Best choices are light, smooth, fruity reds, such as generic Beaujolais, or Bardolino from Italy. These apparently mild-mannered wines are far more likely to succeed with Thai food than tougher numbers, which will simply seem aggressive, charmless, and hot.

Any young red made for quick consumption is likely to work well. Production method, in this case, is more important than grape variety. A quick look at the alcohol level is likely to give a clue to suitability. Aim for something under 12 percent by volume. Choose wines with striking fruit rather than anything more complex; there are plenty of Australian wines with a great deal to offer here. As with the whites, avoid anything aged in oak. You might look out for anything made with the Gamay grape variety, or the lighter, cheerier styles of Californian Zinfandel or South African Pinotage, or even Rioja Tinto Sin Crianza—a new-style, unoaked red Rioja. Finally, don't overlook the much-maligned and unfairly neglected rosé!

In general, don't be browbeaten into choosing some macho wine "capable of standing up to the challenge." What you are looking for is something compatible, not combative. Delicate wines have some delightful surprises in store here: especially those unfashionable enough to retain a trace of sweetness. The Thais themselves have recently started growing grapes in their northern hills, where once only opium poppies blew in secluded valleys. It will be interesting to see what develops.

Snacks & Appetizers

Most of these snacks are really street food, and are still sold on street corners and in marketplaces all over Thailand to satisfy all sorts of appetites, from the hungry schoolchild to the farmer or the Bangkok businessman who needs a quick breakfast or lunch. In other words, they are casual snacks that you can eat at any time. When they appear at table, it is as side dishes or accompaniments to a traditional Thai meal where there are many members of the family present or many guests. All the food is served at once, displayed on a large table so that people can help themselves.

Thai people love deep-fried food, and if you meet these dishes in Bangkok you may sometimes find them rather oily; but the message is getting through, in Thailand as elsewhere, that too much fat is not good for you. I steam everything I can, and where frying is necessary I shallow-fry in as little oil as possible. Of course, if you are not worried about fat levels, you can still deep-fry the Spring Rolls or Golden Bags; and remember that carefully deep-fried food cooked at the right temperature does not absorb much oil.

Go easy on the salt, too: Thai fish sauce is already quite salty enough, and when I say "Taste, and adjust the seasoning" I do mean that you should taste what's cooking before adding any extra salt—you probably won't need it. An old-fashioned Thai cookbook will also tell you to put lots of sugar into many of these dishes, because Thais have a sweet tooth. I have reduced the sugar content of all these recipes drastically.

In spite of these little changes in the name of health and long life, you will find that all these dishes taste at least as good as they do in their homeland.

Miniature Spring Rolls and Tofu and Pomelo on Lettuce Leaves (pages 32-33)

POPIA SOHT
Miniature Spring Rolls

These miniature, canapé-sized spring rolls (see previous page) are the ones that Thais themselves prefer. In Thai restaurants overseas they are always part of the appetizer menu. You can buy them ready-made from the freezer in Thai food shops, but these are usually only suitable for frying. Homemade spring rolls can be steamed, which is healthier and tastes just as good. The two standard fillings are minced pork, or, as here, a vegetarian mixture.

If you prefer, you can deep-fry the spring rolls in hot peanut oil, 6 to 8 at a time, for 2 to 3 minutes per batch, until golden brown.

MAKES 50

PREPARATION
*about 35 minutes,
plus 15 minutes'
soaking*
COOKING
*about 20 minutes,
plus cooling*

Calories per roll *44*
Total fat *1 g (25%)*
Saturated fat *0.5 g*
Protein *1 g*
Carbohydrate *7 g*
Cholesterol *5 mg*
Vitamins *A, C, Folic Acid*
Minerals *Potassium*

1 package of 50 spring roll wrappers, each 5 inches square

For the filling:
3½-ounce package of cellophane vermicelli
½ ounce wood ear mushrooms
4 dried shiitake mushrooms
2 tablespoons vegetable oil
5 medium carrots, peeled and grated or cut into tiny matchsticks
8 ounces green beans or snow peas, cut into thin slices
4 ounces white cabbage leaves, very finely shredded

6 ounces canned bamboo shoots, cut into tiny matchsticks
1 teaspoon salt
½ teaspoon freshly ground black pepper
3 tablespoons finely chopped scallions
½-inch piece of fresh ginger, finely chopped
2 tablespoons light soy sauce
1 egg, separated

To serve:
crisp lettuce leaves
Sweet Chili Sauce (page 142)
whole red chili peppers (optional)
sprigs of mint (optional)

1 Allow the spring roll wrappers to thaw completely in the refrigerator. When thawed, single wrappers can (with care) easily be peeled off from the rest. Stack the loose wrappers on a plate—once they are unstuck, they won't stick together again. Cover with a damp cloth. Set aside in a cool place or in the refrigerator while preparing the filling.

2 Soak the cellophane vermicelli in hot water for 5 minutes, and drain. Using scissors, cut it into short lengths (3 to 4 inches). At the same time, in separate bowls, soak the wood ear and shiitake mushrooms in very hot water just to cover for 15 minutes. Drain; remove and discard the shiitake stalks, then slice the mushrooms thinly.

3 Heat the oil in a wok or frying pan and stir-fry the vegetables: first the carrots, then the beans, cabbage, and bamboo shoots. Season with salt and pepper. Continue stir-frying for about 4 minutes, then add the rest of the ingredients except the egg. Simmer, stirring often, for another 3 minutes.

Remove from heat, cover, and leave to cool.

4   When the filling has cooled, taste and adjust the seasoning. Now add the egg yolk, stir, and mix well. Save the white of the egg in a small bowl, beat it lightly, and set aside.

5   Start rolling the spring rolls. Lay a wrapper on a flat surface, and put about 2 teaspoonfuls of filling on the corner nearest to you. Fold this corner over the filling, and roll the wrapper with the filling inside it halfway to the far corner, which now sticks out like the flap of an envelope. Then fold the other two corners toward the center, brush the envelope flap with egg white, and fold it so that the roll is sealed.

Repeat until all the rolls are made and sealed—all as nearly as possible the same size and shape.

6   If you are not going to serve all the rolls now, pack some in food storage containers, separating the layers of rolls with plastic wrap. Put lids on the containers and freeze; the rolls will keep for about 2 months.

7   Arrange the rolls in a single layer on a plate, and steam in a double saucepan or a vegetable steamer for 5 to 6 minutes.

8   Serve hot with crisp lettuce leaves and Sweet Chili Sauce. If you like, garnish with whole red chilies and mint leaves. To eat, wrap each one in a lettuce leaf, then dip it into the sauce.

TOFU AND POMELO ON LETTUCE LEAVES

This is a variation on the Pomelo and Crab Salad on page 54, but served here as a canapé, on lettuce leaves (see page 31).

1 pomelo
14-16 ounces firm Chinese-style tofu
2 tablespoons peanut oil
1 tablespoon light soy sauce
firm-leaved lettuce, to serve

For the dressing:
2-4 small red bird chilies, thinly sliced

1 tablespoon chopped palm sugar or brown granulated sugar
1 tablespoon nam pla fish sauce
1 teaspoon light soy sauce
3 tablespoons mild rice vinegar or lime juice
1 tablespoon chopped cilantro leaves
1 small shallot, finely chopped
4 scallions, thinly sliced
3 tablespoons warm water

SERVES 4-6

PREPARATION
*about 15 minutes,
plus 10 minutes'
soaking and draining*
COOKING
about 5 minutes

Calories per serving *336*
Total fat *15 g (41%)*
Saturated fat *1 g*
Protein *33 g*
Carbohydrate *23 g*
Cholesterol *None*
Vitamins *B12,
Folic Acid, C*
Minerals *Calcium,
Potassium, Iron, Zinc*

1   Peel and segment the pomelo (see page 12), and separate the segments into small clusters.

2   Put the tofu in a bowl, pour over boiling water to cover and leave for 10 minutes, then drain it and cut into 16 cubes. Cut the cubes in half, then drain these pieces in a colander for a few minutes more.

3   Heat the oil in a nonstick frying pan and carefully

sauté the tofu pieces for 2 to 3 minutes until crisp and golden. Add the soy sauce, mix well, then drain again in a colander.

4   Mix all the dressing ingredients in a small bowl.

5   Put the pomelo and tofu in a larger bowl, pour the dressing over them, and toss. Serve immediately on lettuce leaves.

CRAB CAKES

MAKES ABOUT 12

PREPARATION
*about 15 minutes,
plus 30 minutes'
resting*
COOKING
about 15 minutes

Calories per serving *272*
Total fat *15 g (48%)*
Saturated fat *3 g*
Protein *25 g*
Carbohydrate *11 g*
Cholesterol *188 mg*
Vitamins *B group, E*
Minerals *Potassium, Iron,
Zinc, Selenium, Iodine*

*white and brown meat of 2 medium-sized crabs,
total weight about 1 pound or a little less*
3 scallions, thinly sliced
¼ teaspoon medium-hot chili powder
¼ teaspoon ground white pepper
2 tablespoons chopped cilantro leaves
½-inch piece of fresh ginger, finely chopped
¼ teaspoon ground turmeric
1 teaspoon ground coriander

2 teaspoons finely chopped lemongrass
1 teaspoon baking powder
2 teaspoons lime juice
1 teaspoon sugar
1 teaspoon salt, or more to taste
1 tablespoon all-purpose flour or rice flour
2 eggs, separated
4 tablespoons fine breadcrumbs
2 tablespoons vegetable oil

1 Put the crabmeat in a bowl with all the other ingredients except the eggs, breadcrumbs, and oil. Lightly beat the egg yolks and stir them in. Mix everything well together by hand. Divide the mixture into 12 portions and mold each portion into a ball. Leave to rest in the refrigerator for 30 minutes.

2 Heat the oil in a large nonstick frying pan. Flatten each crab ball to make a round cake, dip it in the lightly beaten egg whites, then sprinkle it with breadcrumbs. Fry the cakes, a few at a time, in the hot oil for 2 minutes on each side, turning once. Drain them on paper towels. Serve immediately.

FISH SATAY

SERVES 10
*as an appetizer, or 4
as a main course*

PREPARATION
*about 20 minutes,
plus marinating*
COOKING
about 5 minutes

Calories per serving *130*
Total fat *4 g (28%)*
Saturated fat *2 g*
Protein *22 g*
Carbohydrate *2 g*
Cholesterol *35 mg*
Vitamins *B12, E*
Minerals *Potassium,
Iodine*

If you use bamboo skewers, soak them thoroughly in water beforehand so that they don't burn.

2¼ pounds boned monkfish tail or halibut steak

For the marinade:
1-inch piece of galingale, finely chopped
1 teaspoon finely chopped lemongrass
4 cilantro roots, chopped
3 shallots, chopped

3 garlic cloves, chopped
2 small fresh or dried chilies, chopped
2 tablespoons chopped creamed coconut
½ cup hot water
juice of 1 small lime
1 teaspoon salt

1 Put all the marinade ingredients in a blender and blend until smooth. Transfer to a bowl.
2 Cut the fish into bite-sized pieces. Mix into the marinade and leave in a cool place or in the refrigerator for 30 minutes or up to 2 hours. Take

out of the refrigerator 30 minutes before you want to cook. Put 2 to 4 pieces on each of 20 bamboo or metal skewers, and rub with the marinade.
3 Preheat a grill or broiler and grill or broil the skewers for 2 minutes on each side, turning once.

Crab Cakes and Fish Satay served on a bed of mixed salad leaves with Cucumber Relish (page 144)

STEAMED FISH DUMPLINGS

When fish dumplings are eaten as a snack, the usual way is to pick up a dumpling with a piece of lettuce leaf, then dip it in a hot-and-sour or sweet-and-sour dip and pop it in your mouth. They can also be served in soup, or cut into slices to garnish a salad made with cellophane noodles or rice vermicelli. Alternatively, serve them as a first course with Cucumber Relish (page 144) and some salad leaves.

1 pound cod, sea bass, or ocean perch fillets, cubed
8 ounces raw jumbo shrimp, shelled, deveined, and chopped
2 tablespoons chopped scallions
large pinch of ground white pepper
1 teaspoon nam pla fish sauce
1 teaspoon light soy sauce
1 teaspoon cornstarch, diluted in 1 tablespoon of cold water

1 egg white, lightly beaten
1 tablespoon lime or lemon juice
salt

To serve:
lettuce leaves
Sweet Chili Sauce (page 142)

MAKES ABOUT 12-16

PREPARATION
about 30 minutes
COOKING
about 15 minutes

Calories per dumpling *36*
Total fat *0.3 g (8%)*
Saturated fat *None*
Protein *8 g*
Carbohydrate *0.5 g*
Cholesterol *40 mg*
Vitamins *B12*
Minerals *Potassium*

1   Put all the ingredients for the dumplings, except the egg white and lime or lemon juice, into a food processor or blender with a large pinch of salt. Blend for a few seconds. Transfer the mixture to a bowl, then add the egg white and stir with a wooden spoon or a fork in one direction only (it doesn't matter which), until the mixture thickens and becomes difficult to stir. This will take about 2 minutes.

2   Half fill a saucepan with water and bring it to a boil. Add the lime or lemon juice and 1 teaspoon of salt. Take 2 dessert spoons, plunge them into a bowl of cold water to wet them, then scoop up a spoonful of the mixture. Mold it between the bowls of the spoons to form an egg-shaped dumpling—a quenelle. Plunge it into the boiling water, count to

five, and remove with a slotted spoon. Drain in a colander. Repeat until all the mixture is used.

3   To be served as snacks or a first course, or to garnish a noodle salad, the dumplings must be steamed. Put them all in a deep plate that will go into your steamer, and steam them for 3 minutes. If you have no steamer, use a large saucepan with a trivet or other support at the bottom. The water should come up only to the top of the trivet. When it boils, put the plate of dumplings on the trivet, cover the pan, and steam for 3 minutes. Serve hot with lettuce leaves and sauce as suggested above.

4   If using the dumplings in a soup, the steaming is unnecessary. Just put the poached dumplings in the broth, simmer for 3 minutes, and serve.

DRY-FRIED SHRIMP

In Thailand, this dish is made with small fresh shrimps, cleaned and with their heads removed but with shells and tails intact. They taste hot and sweet and crisp as you crunch the whole shrimp, shell and all. Here, however, I use medium-sized peeled cooked shrimp. They are excellent for a cocktail party or a special snack.

2 medium-sized red chilies, seeded and chopped
1 garlic clove, chopped
½ teaspoon coarse salt
½ cup hot water
2 tablespoons chopped cilantro leaves
2 teaspoons chopped cilantro roots

2 tablespoons grated palm sugar, demerara, or brown granulated sugar
1-2 teaspoons nam pla fish sauce
about 30 peeled cooked shrimp
1 tablespoon lime juice

SERVES UP TO 10

PREPARATION
about 20 minutes
COOKING
about 15 minutes

1 In a mortar with a pestle, crush the chilies and garlic with the salt. Transfer to a wok or pan.
2 Add the hot water and the rest of the ingredients except the shrimp and the lime juice. Cook the chili mixture for 8 to 10 minutes over medium heat.

3 When the mixture is thick and the sugar starts to caramelize, add the shrimp and stir quickly for 30 seconds. Stir in the lime juice.
4 Transfer to a serving dish. Serve hot or warm, with toothpicks on the side for picking up the shrimp.

Calories per serving *13*
Total fat *0.1 g (9%)*
Saturated fat *None*
Protein *3 g*
Carbohydrate *0.5 g*
Cholesterol *28 mg*
Vitamins *A, B12*
Minerals *Potassium, Selenium, Iodine*

TANG TONG
Golden Bags

They are called "golden" because the finished dish should be a nice golden color. Call them money bags if you like, and create your own filling. The traditional Thai golden bags are made of dried tofu sheets. As these are not always available in the West, I use wonton skins instead. If you prefer, you can deep-fry the bags in medium-hot peanut oil, 4 at a time, for 4 to 5 minutes per batch, until golden brown.

6-8 ounces wonton skins
20-24 chive stalks, soaked in hot water for 5 minutes, then drained

For the filling:
½ skinless chicken breast (about 4-5 ounces)
4 ounces raw shrimp, shelled and deveined
2 ounces water chestnuts, chopped

3 scallions, thinly sliced
2 garlic cloves, chopped
2-inch piece of fresh ginger, finely chopped
1 tablespoon nam pla fish sauce
1 tablespoon chopped cilantro leaves
½ teaspoon freshly ground pepper
¼ teaspoon salt
1 small egg, lightly beaten

MAKES 20-24

PREPARATION
about 40 minutes
COOKING
6-8 minutes

Calories per bag *20*
Total fat *0.4 g (18%)*
Saturated fat *0.1 g*
Protein *3 g*
Carbohydrate *2 g*
Cholesterol *22 mg*
Vitamins *B12*
Minerals *Potassium*

1 First make the filling: mince the chicken and chop the shrimp. Put all the ingredients in a bowl and mix them well. Fry a teaspoonful of the mixture to taste the seasoning. Add more salt or fish sauce if needed.
2 Divide the filling among the wonton squares, piling it in the middle. Gather the four corners of

each square and tie them with a chive stalk above the filling, like a little bag.
3 Arrange the bags in a single layer on a plate, and steam in a double saucepan or a vegetable steamer for 5 to 6 minutes. Serve hot, warm, or cold, with a chili sauce as a dip if you wish.

Overleaf: Golden Bags on a bed of lettuce leaves and Dry-fried Shrimp

SPICY SHRIMP ON MIANG LEAVES

Miang leaves (Piper sarmentosum) *can be bought in Thai grocery shops in small packets of about 4 to 6 ounces. Wash them thoroughly, then dry them with a cloth or with paper towels. Kept in a plastic bag in the refrigerator, they will stay fresh for about a week. Miang leaves are believed to have beneficial medicinal properties and are often used in Thailand to make a calming infusion. If you find miang leaves an acquired taste, or simply cannot get them, wrap the shrimp in radicchio or endive.*

SERVES 4
as a snack or first course

PREPARATION
about 25 minutes
COOKING
about 8 minutes, plus cooling

Calories per serving *112*
Total fat *4 g (34%)*
Saturated fat *2 g*
Protein *15 g*
Carbohydrate *4 g*
Cholesterol *135 mg*
Vitamins *A, B group, C, E*
Minerals *Calcium, Iron, Zinc, Selenium, Iodine*

8 ounces small peeled cooked shrimp, rinsed in cold water
2 teaspoons finely chopped lemongrass
3-5 small red bird chilies, finely chopped
½ kaffir lime or unwaxed lime, finely diced with the peel, seeds discarded
2-inch piece of fresh ginger, preferably young, or pickled ginger
pinch of salt
12 or 16 miang leaves, or radicchio or endive leaves

For the sauce:
¾-inch piece of fresh galingale, peeled and finely chopped

1 tablespoon freshly grated or desiccated coconut
2 tablespoons dried shrimps
1 teaspoon shrimp paste (kapi)
1 tablespoon palm sugar, demerara, or brown granulated sugar
2 tablespoons nam pla fish sauce

For the garnish:
1 tablespoon chopped roasted peanuts (optional)
handful of cilantro leaves
2-3 scallions, sliced at an angle
2-3 small red chilies, seeded and thinly sliced (optional)

1 In a bowl, stir together the cooked shrimp, lemongrass, chilies, lime, ginger, and salt. Set aside.

2 Make the sauce: put the chopped galingale and the coconut in a wok, set over a low heat, and roast, stirring all the time, for 3 minutes or until the coconut turns golden. Add the dried shrimps and the shrimp paste. Stir for another minute, then add the rest of the ingredients for the sauce along with ½ cup water. Simmer for 2 to 3 minutes and remove from heat. Leave to cool.

3 When the sauce has cooled, pour it into the bowl of cooked shrimp and other ingredients. Mix well.

4 To serve: lay the miang, radicchio, or endive leaves on plates, and spoon equal amounts of the shrimp mixture on each leaf. Sprinkle the garnish over all and serve. I much prefer to eat these shrimp by rolling or wrapping them in the leaves and eating them with my fingers.

Spicy Shrimp on Miang Leaves

Soups

In Thailand, as in many other Asian countries, a bowl of soup is placed on the table at the beginning of the meal and stays there till the end, ready to be spooned into your plate whenever you need liquid to wash the food down. We do not normally expect any other long drink, because you can quickly feel bloated if you drink a lot of water with rice or noodles, and then you won't enjoy the meal. Hence the advantage of drinking wine rather than beer to accompany Thai food (see page 28).

Any of the soups in this book can be served in the Thai way, or as a single course in your own menu. The recipes suggest different ways of serving them. Remember that some Thai soups are hot and sour; if you have anyone at your table who is very sensitive to chilies, you may need to cut down on the chili in the soup or leave it out altogether—otherwise he will need something else to drink to keep his throat cool.

Most of the soup recipes in this section include ingredients and instructions for the appropriate stock. However, as a general guide I also give here the recipes for four basic stocks, to which you can add whatever other ingredients you like, to give a Thai flavor to any soup. Your soup does not need to be limited to Thai ingredients, but you will have the taste of Thailand in the stock.

You can, of course, add other seasonings and flavors, such as a little more chili or chili oil, more tamarind water or lime juice, salt and pepper, fish sauce or soy sauce, just before you serve the soup. Likewise you can add basil leaves, cilantro leaves, and the chopped inner soft part of lemongrass, or coconut milk or creamed coconut.

Hot-and-Sour Stock (page 44) in preparation

BASIC THAI VEGETABLE STOCK

MAKES ABOUT
1¾ PINTS

PREPARATION
about 5 minutes
COOKING
30-40 minutes

5 cups cold water
1 small onion, quartered, or 2 shallots, whole or coarsely chopped

1 stalk of lemongrass, cut into 3 pieces
¾-inch piece of galingale, sliced
½ teaspoon salt

1 Put all the ingredients in a large saucepan. Bring to the boil and simmer gently for 30 to 40 minutes, skimming as necessary. Then strain the stock into another saucepan and discard the solids.

2 You can, of course, add more water and seasoning to this basic stock.

THAI CHICKEN STOCK

You can make the basic vegetable stock in one saucepan and chicken stock, from chicken skins and bones, in another. Combine the two when you know how much liquid you are going to need. Alternatively, you can put about ½ pound chicken trimmings, bones, and skin, into the basic stock right from the start. If you prefer, skim off any fat that rises to the surface.

THAI SEAFOOD STOCK

About 15 minutes before you finish cooking the basic vegetable stock, add about ½ pound shrimp shells or fish heads and bones as appropriate. Alternatively, boil the shells or bones separately for 10 minutes, then mix with the basic vegetable stock and continue simmering for another 10 minutes.

HOT-AND-SOUR STOCK

Whether this is made from a base of just vegetable stock or chicken or seafood stock, about 10 minutes before the stock finishes cooking, add 2 tablespoonfuls of tamarind water or lime juice and 2 to 4 red chilies whole or cut in half. The chili taste will remain, without your soup becoming too hot. (See previous page.)

CLEAR BROTH OF MUSHROOMS WITH EGGS AND CARROTS

For generations, cooks in the East have been putting quails' eggs or very small hens' eggs into soup. Here, the impression of "something special" can be heightened by slicing the peeled and appropriately grooved carrots very thinly into flower-petal shapes. The water used to rehydrate the powerfully flavored dried mushrooms is the only stock required for the soup.

1 medium-sized carrot, peeled and sliced
salt and pepper
8 quails' eggs or 4 small hens' eggs, soft-boiled (1-2 minutes for quails' eggs, 3-4 minutes for hens')
4-8 leaves of flat-leaf parsley or cilantro

For the broth:
1 ounce dried porcini (cèpes) or dried shiitake mushrooms
2 tablespoons vegetable oil
8 ounces button mushrooms, diced
1 garlic clove, crushed
½-inch piece of fresh ginger

SERVES 4

PREPARATION *about 15 minutes, plus 20 minutes' soaking*
COOKING *about 40 minutes*

Calories per serving *180*
Total fat *13 g (63%)*
Saturated fat *3 g*
Protein *10 g*
Carbohydrate *7 g*
Cholesterol *540 mg*
Vitamins *A, B group, E*
Minerals *Potassium, Iron*

1 Soak the dried mushrooms in hot water for 20 minutes. Drain, reserving liquid; remove stalks from mushrooms. Put the stalks and soaking liquid, together with 4 cups water, into a saucepan. Dice the cèpes or shiitakes.

2 In a wok or frying pan, heat the oil and stir-fry the diced cèpes or shiitakes and the button mushrooms for 2 to 3 minutes. Add the garlic and ginger, and transfer the mixture to the saucepan. Bring to a boil and simmer for 20 minutes.

3 Strain the broth through a sieve into another saucepan. Bring the broth back to a simmer and add the sliced carrots, salt, and pepper. Continue simmering for another 6 to 8 minutes.

4 Carefully shell the eggs. If you use quails' eggs, these can be left whole or cut in half. Hens' eggs should be halved or quartered. Divide the eggs among the soup plates. Adjust the seasoning of the broth, then ladle it, piping hot, over the eggs, and garnish with parsley or cilantro leaves.

CLEAR SOUP OF CHICKEN AND MUSHROOMS

This is a variation on the Clear Broth of Mushrooms with Eggs and Carrots on the previous page. Chicken soup is universally acclaimed as being good for you, and to its other virtues the Thais have added what they regard as a health-giving rhizome, galingale or, in the Thai language, ka.

SERVES 4-6

PREPARATION
*about 15 minutes,
plus 20 minutes'
soaking*
COOKING
about 1 hour

Calories per serving *149*
Total fat *8 g (47%)*
Saturated fat *2 g*
Protein *14 g*
Carbohydrate *6 g*
Cholesterol *42 mg*
Vitamins *B group*
Minerals *Potassium, Iron,
Zinc, Selenium*

1 ounce dried cèpes or shiitake mushrooms
2 tablespoons vegetable oil
½ pound button mushrooms, diced
1 garlic clove, crushed
2-inch piece of fresh galingale, sliced
1 whole chicken breast, with skin and bones

*4 ounces fresh shiitake or chestnut mushrooms,
thinly sliced, or halved if very small*
salt and pepper
juice of ½ lime
4-8 leaves of flat-leaf parsley or cilantro

1 Soak the dried mushrooms in hot water for 20 minutes. Drain, reserving liquid; remove stalks from mushrooms. Put the stalks and the soaking water into a saucepan, together with 5 cups of water. Dice the cèpes or shiitake. In a wok or frying pan, heat the oil and stir-fry the diced cèpes or shiitake mushrooms and the diced button mushrooms for 2 to 3 minutes. Add the garlic and galingale and transfer the mixture to the saucepan. Bring to a boil, add the chicken breasts, and simmer for 10 minutes.

2 Remove the chicken breasts from the stock. Skin and bone them, and put the skin and bones back into the pot. Continue to simmer the stock for 30 minutes. Strain the broth into another saucepan through a cheesecloth-lined sieve. If you prefer, skim off any fat from the surface of the stock.

3 Slice the chicken breast into bite-sized pieces and set aside. Bring the clear broth back to a simmer, and add the sliced chicken, the sliced fresh mushrooms, and some salt and pepper. Continue to simmer for another 6 to 8 minutes.

4 Adjust the seasoning. Add the lime juice and parsley or cilantro leaves and serve the soup at once, while piping hot.

Clear Soup of Chicken and Mushrooms

CHICKEN AND RICE SOUP

This healthy soup can provide an excellent means of finishing off leftovers of boiled rice and roast chicken, or you can make it from scratch with everything fresh. This is the fresh version.

SERVES 4-6

PREPARATION
about 15 minutes
COOKING
about 1 hour

Calories per serving *144*
Total fat *4 g (23%)*
Saturated fat *1 g*
Protein *13 g*
Carbohydrate *15 g*
Cholesterol *36 mg*
Vitamins *B group*
Minerals *Potassium, Iron, Selenium, Iodine*

3 ounces jasmine rice, washed and drained
12-18 small button mushrooms, halved
handful of Asian celery leaves or flat-leaved parsley
2 tablespoons chopped cilantro leaves
nam pla fish sauce to taste

For the stock:
1 quantity Basic Thai Vegetable Stock (page 44)
1 whole chicken breast on the bone and with skin

1 Make the stock as described on page 44, adding the chicken breast at the beginning. Simmer for 10 minutes only. Take out the chicken breast, and skin and bone it. Put the skin and bones back into the pot. Shred the meat by hand or chop it, and set aside.
2 Bring the stock back to a boil and simmer for 20 minutes. Strain the stock through a cheesecloth-lined sieve into another saucepan. Discard the solids.

3 If you prefer, skim off any fat from the surface of the stock. Bring the stock to a boil and add the rice. Boil for 6 minutes. Lower the heat and add the chicken, the mushrooms, and the celery or parsley leaves. Simmer for 5 minutes. Adjust the seasoning with more salt if necessary and add the chopped cilantro leaves and fish sauce to taste. Continue to simmer for 2 minutes more, and serve immediately.

TOM YAM KUNG
Hot-and-Sour Soup with Shrimp

SERVES 4-6

PREPARATION
about 30 minutes
COOKING
about 30 minutes

Calories per serving *23*
Total fat *0.3 g (10%)*
Saturated fat *None*
Protein *3 g*
Carbohydrate *2 g*
Cholesterol *24 mg*
Vitamins *B12*
Minerals *Potassium, Iron, Selenium, Iodine*

All over Southeast Asia you will find variations on hot-and-sour soup. A good one should be clear, not cloudy, and should not be made with a hot-and-sour paste. This is the most popular soup in Thailand.

12-18 large raw shrimp in the shell
12-18 fresh or canned straw mushrooms, or 12-18 small button mushrooms
juice of ½ lime
2 tablespoons chopped cilantro leaves
nam pla fish sauce to taste

For the stock:
5 cups water
2-inch piece of fresh galingale, sliced
3 kaffir lime leaves, coarsely shredded
3-4 large red chilies, halved
2 shallots, coarsely chopped
2 stalks of lemongrass, halved
½ teaspoon salt

1 Shell and devein the shrimp. Wash the shells well, and keep them for the stock pot. Slice or quarter the mushrooms. If using canned straw mushrooms,

drain and rinse them first.
2 Put all the ingredients for the stock in a saucepan together with the reserved shrimp shells. Bring to a

boil and simmer for 15 minutes. Strain into another saucepan through a cheesecloth-lined sieve.

3 Bring the clear stock to a boil, then add the shrimp and the mushrooms. Simmer for 4 minutes. Add the lime juice, chopped cilantro leaves, and fish sauce to taste. Serve piping hot.

HOT-AND-SOUR SOUP WITH TOFU

The recipe for this vegetarian soup calls for a small quantity of fermented yellow beans. If, however, you already have some of the Japanese fermented beans called miso, *it can be used instead.*

1 block of Chinese-style tofu, weighing about 12-14 ounces
12-18 small button mushrooms, halved
1 pound young spinach, washed well
juice of ½ lime
2 tablespoons chopped cilantro leaves
salt

For the stock:
5 cups water
1 tablespoon fermented yellow beans or miso
2-inch piece of fresh galingale, sliced
3 kaffir lime leaves, coarsely shredded
3-4 large red chilies, halved
2 shallots, coarsely chopped
2 stalks of lemongrass, halved
½ teaspoon salt

SERVES 4-6

PREPARATION
about 20 minutes
COOKING
about 35 minutes

Calories per serving *269*
Total fat *11 g (36%)*
Saturated fat *None*
Protein *31 g*
Carbohydrate *17 g*
Cholesterol *None*
Vitamins *A, B6, Folic Acid, C, E*
Minerals *Calcium, Potassium*

1 Cut the tofu into quarters, then cut each quarter into quarters again.

2 Put all the ingredients for the stock in a saucepan. Bring to a boil and simmer for 20 minutes. Strain the stock into another saucepan through a cheesecloth-lined sieve. Discard the solids.

3 Bring the clear stock to a boil and add the tofu and mushrooms. Simmer for 5 minutes, then add the spinach, lime juice, chopped cilantro leaves, and more salt if necessary. Continue to simmer for 2 minutes more, and serve immediately.

TOM YAM PLA
Hot-and-Sour Soup with Fish

The stock for this hot-and-sour soup is exactly the same as that for the Hot-and-Sour Soup with Shrimp on pages 48-49 except, of course, that there are no shrimp shells here; instead, we use the bones and head of the fish.

1 medium-sized mahimahi or about 1¼ pounds flounder or sole, filleted and skinned

12-18 fresh or canned straw mushrooms, or 12-18 small button mushrooms

1 pound young spinach, washed well

juice of ½ lime

2 tablespoons chopped cilantro leaves, plus more whole leaves for garnish

nam pla fish sauce to taste

whole red chilies, to garnish (optional)

For the stock:

5 cups water

2-inch piece of fresh galingale, sliced

3 kaffir lime leaves, coarsely shredded

3-4 large red chilies, halved lengthwise

2 shallots, coarsely chopped

2 stalks of lemongrass, halved

½ teaspoon salt

SERVES 4-6

PREPARATION
about 20 minutes
COOKING
about 25 minutes

Calories per serving *106*
Total fat *2 g (18%)*
Saturated fat *0.3 g*
Protein *20 g*
Carbohydrate *2 g*
Cholesterol *42 mg*
Vitamins *A, B group, C, E*
Minerals *Calcium, Iron, Zinc, Selenium, Iodine, Potassium*

1   Make sure you get the fishmonger to give you the bones, skin, and, if possible, the head of the fish for the stock. Slice or quarter the mushrooms. If using canned straw mushrooms, drain and rinse them first.

2   Put all the stock ingredients in a saucepan together with the fish trimmings. Bring to a boil and simmer for 15 minutes. Strain into another saucepan through a cheesecloth-lined sieve. Discard the solids.

3   Bring the clear stock to a boil, then add the fish fillets and the mushrooms. Simmer for 3 minutes, then add the spinach, lime juice, chopped cilantro leaves, and fish sauce to taste. Continue to simmer for 1 more minute, and serve immediately, garnished with cilantro leaves and some whole red chilies for color if you like.

Hot-and-Sour Soup with Fish

Salads

The Thai word yam *means "salad," but a Thai salad is not a mere side dish; it is more like a complete meal on a small scale. Noodles, fruit, vegetables, cooked meat, perhaps poultry or fish—this may not sound like a salad at all, if your understanding of the concept does not go much further than mixtures of leaves. However, the whole Thai approach to food leads to dishes that cannot be given any other name: wherever we come from, we associate salads with ingredients that are fresh, light, crisp, sour, and—as far as possible—in their natural state.*

The recipes in this section are Thai, but I use some fruit and salad leaves that are not usually found in a real Thai yam, *for example the combination of avocado and oranges, and the use of arugula and lamb's lettuce, which are fashionable in the West and easily obtainable. The Thais themselves use papaya and mango—usually unripe—and pomelo in savory dishes, but when I do the same I use the fully ripened fruit. Once even the most traditionalist of Thais has tasted the results, I am sure they will soon get used to the idea that ripe mango, sweet pomelo, and ripe papaya are exactly right with seafood.*

Almost all these salads are versatile—I have suggested that one should be served as a snack or appetizer, another as a first course, a third as a main course or a one-dish lunch, but you will see at once that most can be adapted to fill any of these roles.

Pomelo and Crab Salad (page 54) on a bed of mixed green salad leaves and herbs

POMELO AND CRAB SALAD

SERVES 4
*as a first course or 2
as a light lunch*

PREPARATION
about 20 minutes

Calories per serving *154*
Total fat *5 g (29%)*
Saturated fat *0.6 g*
Protein *18 g*
Carbohydrate *10 g*
Cholesterol *63 mg*
Vitamins *B group, C*
Minerals *Potassium, Iron,
Zinc, Selenium*

For the sake of flavor and texture, use fresh crab if you can possibly get it (though top-quality canned crabmeat will do at a pinch). Use only the white meat. If you buy ready-cooked crab from the fishmonger, ask him to open the shell and discard the bits that are not edible. Do not be tempted to buy crab already dressed, because the dressing used in other countries is completely different from Thai dressing.

Serve this salad as a first course, garnished with slices of firm red plum tomatoes, or as a side salad with a combination of green salad leaves (see previous page).

1 pomelo, peeled and segmented and the segments separated into small clusters (see page 12)
12-14 ounces cooked crabmeat (white meat only)

For the dressing:
2-4 small red bird chilies or small dried chilies, finely chopped
1 tablespoon chopped palm sugar or soft brown sugar

1 tablespoon nam pla fish sauce
1 teaspoon light soy sauce
3 tablespoons mild rice vinegar or lime juice
1 tablespoon chopped cilantro leaves
1 small shallot, finely chopped
4 scallions, cleaned and thinly sliced
3 tablespoons warm water

1   Mix all the dressing ingredients in a small bowl.
2   Put the pomelo segments and crabmeat in a larger bowl, pour the dressing into it, and toss.
3   Serve the salad immediately.

POMELO, SHRIMP, AND SCALLOP SALAD

SERVES 4
as a first course

PREPARATION
about 20 minutes
COOKING
about 2 minutes

Calories per serving *144*
Total fat *1 g (8%)*
Saturated fat *0.3 g*
Protein *21 g*
Carbohydrate *13 g*
Cholesterol *69 mg*
Vitamins *B group, C*
Minerals *Potassium, Iron,
Zinc, Selenium, Iodine*

The dressing of this salad is accented by palm sugar and chili. Don't overgarnish the salad with too much greenery; I prefer just a few leaves of arugula or lamb's lettuce.

1 pomelo, peeled and segmented (see page 12)
8-12 scallops, without corals, poached in lightly salted water for 2 minutes only, drained, and patted dry
12 cooked peeled jumbo shrimp
handful of arugula or lamb's lettuce leaves

For the dressing:
1 tablespoon grated palm sugar or demerara or brown granulated sugar
3 tablespoons warm water
2-4 small fresh or dried red chilies, finely chopped
1 garlic clove, crushed
4 tablespoons nam pla fish sauce
juice of 2 limes
3 tablespoons chopped cilantro leaves
2 teaspoons finely chopped lemongrass

1 Divide the pomelo segments among 4 plates, arranging them in a cluster in the middle of each plate. Arrange the scallops and shrimp around them, and scatter the green leaves around the edge.

2 Make the dressing: put the sugar and warm water in a glass bowl. Stir until the sugar is dissolved, then add all the other ingredients for the dressing.

3 Everything can be prepared up to 24 hours in advance and kept in the refrigerator. Store the dressing in a separate container. Take the salad and dressing out of the refrigerator about 20 minutes before serving.

4 About 5 minutes before serving, pour equal amounts of the dressing over each plate of salad.

SHRIMP AND PAPAYA SALAD

For salads, Thai people usually prefer the sourness of green papayas or green mangoes to the sweetness of ripe ones. Here, however, as in the Mango Salad with Salmon on page 58, I use ripe fruit. This dish is very quick to prepare and needs no cooking, but do take the trouble to choose and buy the best cooked shrimp you can get. If you buy frozen shrimp, get the ones with shells, allow them to thaw out completely, and shell them yourself.

2 ripe papayas
juice of 1 lime
20-24 medium-sized peeled cooked shrimp
1 cup of just-boiled water

For the dressing:
2 tablespoons warm water

1 teaspoon sugar
1 small red bird chili, finely chopped
1 shallot, thinly sliced
2 scallions, cleaned and thinly sliced
1 tablespoon nam pla fish sauce
juice of 1 lime

SERVES 4
as a first course

PREPARATION
about 15 minutes, plus 10 minutes' marinating

Calories per serving *58*
Total fat *0.3 g (5%)*
Saturated fat *None*
Protein *5 g*
Carbohydrate *9 g*
Cholesterol *53 mg*
Vitamins *A, B12, C*
Minerals *Potassium, Iron, Selenium, Iodine*

1 Halve the papayas and remove the seeds. Immediately pour the lime juice in equal amounts over the 4 papaya halves. Set aside.

2 Put the shelled shrimp in a bowl and pour a cup of just-boiled water over them. After 1 minute, drain the shrimp in a colander.

3 Prepare the dressing: put the warm water and sugar in another bowl. Stir until the sugar is dissolved, then add the rest of the ingredients for the dressing. Mix well; taste and adjust the seasoning with more fish sauce if necessary. Add the shrimp to the dressing and toss. Leave the shrimp marinating in the dressing for up to 10 minutes.

4 Arrange the shrimp on the papaya halves and serve immediately.

SOM TAM
Green Papaya and Carrot Salad

Papaya contains an enzyme called papain, which can be used as a meat tenderizer. The fruit is a good source of vitamin C, and in Asia the leaves—rich in vitamin A—are cooked and eaten as a vegetable. The water that is squeezed from a puree of raw leaves tastes very bitter but is said to be effective in protecting against malaria.

Here I mix unripe green papaya with carrots, to give color as well as to add vitamin A to the dish. Although both red and green chilies contain vitamin C, red chilies are much richer in vitamin A. For vegetarians, omit the dried shrimps in the dressing and replace the fish sauce with light soy sauce.

SERVES 8-10
as an appetizer

PREPARATION
*about 30 minutes,
plus 30 minutes'
soaking and standing*

Calories per serving *35*
Total fat *0.3 g (7%)*
Saturated fat *None*
Protein *1 g*
Carbohydrate *7 g*
Cholesterol *4 mg*
Vitamins *A, Folic Acid, C*
Minerals *Potassium, Iron,
Iodine*

1 or 2 green unripe papayas, peeled, cut open and seeded (about 1 pound)
1 pound peeled carrots
1 tablespoon salt

For the dressing:
2 garlic cloves, crushed
2 green chilies, seeded and thinly sliced
2 red chilies, seeded and finely chopped
1-2 teaspoons sugar
1 tablespoon nam pla fish sauce

2 tablespoons dried shrimps, soaked for 5 minutes in boiling water, then drained and crushed in a mortar with a pestle
juice of 2 limes
¼ teaspoon salt if needed

For the garnish:
salad leaves
8 cherry or baby plum tomatoes, halved
handful of cilantro leaves

1 Cut the flesh of the papaya into chunks. Grate the chunks in a food processor, or slice them thinly with a mandoline and cut them into very fine strips. Do the same with the carrots.

2 The gratings or fine strips of papaya need to be softened with a tablespoonful of salt. Sprinkle the salt over them, leave them for 10 minutes, then rinse well and drain them in a colander.

3 Mix all the ingredients for the dressing, except the salt, in a large glass bowl. Add the papaya and carrots and mix well with the dressing. Taste, and adjust the seasoning. Leave to stand for at least 20 minutes.

4 Serve alongside—or on a bed of—salad leaves, garnished with the halved tomatoes and the cilantro leaves.

Green Papaya and Carrot Salad

YAM MAMUANG
Mango Salad with Salmon

In Thailand, a salad of unripe mangoes is given a chili-hot, sweet-and-sour dressing, and it is not served with fish. I thought a long time ago that ripe mango would go well with salmon, and experience has proved me right—the marriage of colors and tastes is entirely successful, and is Thai in spirit if not in provenance. I use the chili very sparingly here, so that it does not overpower the delicate flavor of the salmon.

This salad can be prepared up to 24 hours in advance. Keep it in the refrigerator, covered with plastic wrap, and take it out 10 minutes before serving.

SERVES 4
*as a first course
or 2 as a light lunch*

PREPARATION
about 20 minutes
COOKING
*about 7 minutes, plus
cooling*

Calories per serving *256*
Total fat *13 g (45%)*
Saturated fat *2 g*
Protein *24 g*
Carbohydrate *12 g*
Cholesterol *56 mg*
Vitamins *A, B group, C, E*
Minerals *Potassium, Iron,
Zinc, Selenium, Iodine*

1 large mango, peeled and cut into julienne strips
½ teaspoon salt
1 tablespoon lime or lemon juice
handful each of lamb's lettuce and arugula leaves
12-14 cilantro or mint leaves
4 salmon fillets, each about 3½-4½ ounces
2 tablespoons peanut oil
2 shallots, thinly sliced
2 garlic cloves, crushed

1 large red chili, seeded and thinly sliced
1 teaspoon finely chopped lemongrass
2-inch piece of fresh ginger, peeled and finely chopped
2 kaffir lime leaves, finely shredded (optional)
1 tablespoon nam pla fish sauce or light soy sauce
2 tablespoons white wine vinegar
3 tablespoons hot water

1 Put the mango strips in a bowl, and sprinkle with the salt and lime or lemon juice. Keep the lettuce, arugula, and cilantro or mint leaves in another bowl.
2 Cut the salmon fillets into halves lengthwise, then cut each piece into 3 thin strips.
3 Heat the oil in a large frying pan and fry all the chopped and sliced aromatic ingredients, stirring all the time, for 2 minutes. Add the fish sauce, vinegar, and water, and simmer for another 2 minutes. Then add the fish, stir it around gently, and cook over low heat for 1 minute only. Remove from the heat, cover the pan, and keep in a cool place for 5 minutes. Uncover and leave to cool.
4 To serve, divide the greens and mango slices among the serving plates, arranging them at the center of each plate. Top with equal shares of the salmon pieces, with the cooking juices poured over them.

Mango Salad with Salmon

YAM PLA MUEK
Squid Salad

Very young squid are best for this salad as, when cut up, they need only 3 minutes' cooking and their texture is less rubbery than that of older squid. In any case, squid pieces must be cooked for only 3 to 4 minutes, whether they are fried or poached. If you overrun that time, the squid will need to be cooked for 40 minutes or longer to make it tender again.

SERVES 4-6
as a first course

PREPARATION
about 20 minutes
COOKING
*3-4 minutes, plus
cooling*

Calories per serving *114*
Total fat *2 g (16%)*
Saturated fat *0.5 g*
Protein *18 g*
Carbohydrate *6 g*
Cholesterol *253 mg*
Vitamins *B group, C, E*
Minerals *Potassium, Iron,
Zinc, Selenium, Iodine*

1½ pounds small squid, cleaned
4 cups water
½ teaspoon salt
1 cucumber, washed, halved lengthwise, seeds scooped out, and flesh cut into thin half-moon shapes

For the dressing:
juice of 1 lime

1 tablespoon nam pla fish sauce
1 tablespoon light soy sauce
2 teaspoons rice vinegar
1-3 small red bird chilies, finely chopped
2 shallots, very finely sliced
2 teaspoons superfine sugar
4 tablespoons warm water
1 tablespoon chopped cilantro leaves
1 tablespoon chopped basil leaves

1 Start by mixing all the ingredients for the dressing, except the cilantro and basil leaves and the salt, in a glass bowl.

2 Cut the squid into pieces. Boil the water with the salt, put the squid in the boiling water, and leave them to cook, with the water just bubbling a little, for 3 to 4 minutes. Drain immediately.

3 While the squid pieces are still warm, put them in the bowl with the dressing and mix well. Let the squid cool before mixing the cilantro, basil leaves, and cucumber slices into the salad. Adjust the seasoning with more salt if necessary. Serve at room temperature.

Previous pages: Caramelized Shallots and Shrimp Salad, and Squid Salad with Fruit

SQUID SALAD WITH FRUIT

Here is the traditional Thai squid salad, but brightened up with avocado and oranges. You'll be surprised, not only at how the two fruits give a salad a facelift, but also at how much they enhance the taste.

12 ounces small squid, thoroughly cleaned
salt
1 large orange
1 ripe avocado
large bunch of mixed salad leaves
handful each of cilantro and mint leaves

For the dressing:
2 tablespoons nam pla fish sauce
2 tablespoons lime juice
2 small red bird chilies, finely chopped
1 teaspoon superfine sugar
2 teaspoons mild vinegar

1 Cut the squid into rings. Boil half a saucepanful of water, add a large pinch of salt, and put the squid rings into the water. Lower the heat and poach the squid for 3 minutes only. Transfer to a colander.

2 In a bowl, mix the ingredients for the dressing and stir in the warm squid. Set aside to cool. Refrigerate if not serving immediately.

3 Take the squid out of the refrigerator at least 20 minutes before serving. Peel and segment the orange, holding it over a bowl to catch the juice. Peel the avocado, cut it in halves, and remove the pit. Then cut each half into 6 slices and put the slices in the bowl with the orange—the juice will help to prevent the avocado from discoloring.

4 Divide the salad and cilantro leaves among 4 plates. Arrange the orange segments and avocado on top of the leaves, then top them with the squid and the dressing. Garnish with mint leaves to serve.

SERVES 4
as a starter

PREPARATION
about 30 minutes
COOKING
about 3 minutes, plus cooling

Calories per serving *174*
Total fat *9 g (46%)*
Saturated fat *2 g*
Protein *15 g*
Carbohydrate *9 g*
Cholesterol *191 mg*
Vitamins *B group, C, E*
Minerals *Potassium, Iron, Zinc, Selenium, Iodine*

CARAMELIZED SHALLOTS AND SHRIMP SALAD

The idea for this dish comes from a traditional Thai dish of prawns and pickled garlic, which needs a lot of sugar to moderate the strong flavor of the garlic. With the caramelized shallots, you need far less sugar.

16 small shallots or Thai small red onions, halved
1 tablespoon sugar
1 tablespoon rice vinegar
1 tablespoon peanut oil
20 peeled cooked jumbo shrimp
1 tablespoon nam pla fish sauce

2 teaspoons fresh or pickled green peppercorns
handful of cilantro leaves
3 tablespoons hot water
2 teaspoons finely chopped lemongrass
½ lime or kaffir lime, finely diced with the peel, discarding all the seeds

1 Put the shallots or onions into a wok or large frying pan with the sugar, vinegar, and oil. Cook over low heat for 12 to 15 minutes, stirring often.

2 Add the shrimp and the fish sauce, stir for 1 minute, then stir in the remaining ingredients. Serve immediately, or let cool to room temperature. To serve as a main course, accompany with sticky rice.

SERVES 4
as a first course

PREPARATION
about 15 minutes
COOKING
15-20 minutes

Calories per serving *122*
Total fat *3 g (25%)*
Saturated fat *0.6 g*
Protein *9 g*
Carbohydrate *15 g*
Cholesterol *73 mg*
Vitamins *B group, C, E*
Minerals *Potassium, Iron, Zinc, Selenium, Iodine*

CURRIED EGG SALAD

The combination of salad ingredients given here is unusual, so feel free to substitute or add whatever is to your taste. The curry sauce that goes with the salad needs to be quite concentrated and thick. I suggest using one-third of the quantity shown on page 116 for the standard curry paste, either the green or the red. If you have curry paste cubes in your freezer, equivalent to one tablespoonful each, then use 6 cubes.

SERVES 4

PREPARATION
about 20 minutes
COOKING
*about 10 minutes,
plus the eggs*

Calories per serving *280*
Total fat *16 g (53%)*
Saturated fat *5 g*
Protein *19 g*
Carbohydrate *16 g*
Cholesterol *406 mg*
Vitamins *A, B group, C, E*
Minerals *Calcium, Iron,
Zinc, Selenium, Iodine*

6-8 hens' or ducks' eggs
⅓ quantity standard green or red curry paste, or
6 frozen curry paste cubes (page 116)
7 tablespoons low-fat plain yogurt
1 teaspoon sugar (optional)
1 teaspoon lime juice
salt
1 ripe but still firm mango, peeled and cubed
2 white cabbage leaves, very finely shredded

1 bunch of watercress, trimmed
4 small round eggplants, quartered, or ½ cucumber, peeled and cubed
1 small green chili, chopped (optional)
1 teaspoon finely chopped lemongrass
2 tablespoons finely chopped cilantro leaves
¼ teaspoon salt
1 teaspoon nam pla fish sauce (optional)

1 Hard-boil the eggs and let them cool.

2 Put the curry paste or cubes into a saucepan, bring nearly to a boil, and simmer, stirring often, for 3 minutes. Add 5 tablespoons of the yogurt, the sugar if needed, the lime juice, and salt. Continue simmering for 4 minutes, stirring once or twice. Adjust the seasoning. Turn off the heat.

3 Shell and quarter the eggs, and mix them gently into the thick curry sauce. Do not break them up

too much—you want the largest possible fragments.

4 Put all the remaining ingredients for the salad into a bowl and mix well. Serve at room temperature, dividing the salad among 4 plates and arranging equal amounts of the curried egg on top. Alternatively, you can omit mixing the eggs into the curry sauce, and just pour the sauce over the eggs and salad at the end.

Curried Egg Salad

Fish & Shellfish

Many of my friends in the West call themselves "vegetarians," but eat fish. This has never seemed to me remarkable; our Asian diet has always been based on vegetables, fruit, and fish. Most Asians have lived for centuries—and often lived rather well—on what they could gather from the earth and waters around them. Vegetables and fruit came from their own tiny patches of land, fish and shrimp from the ponds that most people own in the villages. There were more fish in the rivers and the flooded rice fields. Most of them lived quite near the coast and could buy dried, salted fish. This was perhaps the best protein source of all, as well as being the food that would keep them alive when flood, drought, or war ruined their crops.

Fish are not yet an industrial product, though they seem to be going that way. For the moment, most fish that come fresh to market have been caught fairly close to where they are sold. The result is that species familiar to me in Southeast Asia may be unobtainable elsewhere. However, I have never had any difficulty in finding a fish to suit my purpose in any part of the world. Some of my most colorful memories are of fish markets, in Indonesia and Thailand of course, but also on the Rialto in Venice, in Sydney, and in frosty, windy dawns in Philadelphia and London.

Minced Fish on Lemongrass Sticks (page 68)

MINCED FISH ON LEMONGRASS STICKS

SERVES 4
as first course or 8 as snacks with drinks

PREPARATION
about 30 minutes, plus 30 minutes' chilling
COOKING
about 4 minutes

Calories per serving *111*
Total fat *1 g (7%)*
Saturated fat *0.1 g*
Protein *22 g*
Carbohydrate *4 g*
Cholesterol *52 mg*
Vitamins *B group*
Minerals *Potassium, Selenium, Iodine*

Traditionally this minced fish is deep-fried, but here is a healthier version: the fish is grilled and served with steamed rice, or simply with Cucumber Relish or Chili and Green Mango Relish (page 144). The texture of the fish is better if it is finely chopped with a knife rather than in a food processor. (See previous page.)

1 pound cod, halibut, or ocean perch fillets, finely chopped
2 shallots, finely chopped
2 teaspoons finely chopped cilantro roots
1 teaspoon finely chopped red chilies
1 tablespoon nam pla fish sauce

1 tablespoon lime juice
1 teaspoon sugar
large pinch of salt
1 egg white, lightly beaten
8 short lemongrass stems, trimmed
cilantro leaves, to garnish

1 Put all the ingredients except the egg white and lemongrass in a large bowl. Mix well, by hand or with a fork. Add the egg white and mix it in with a fork, in one direction only, until the mixture becomes difficult to turn. Form the mixture into 8 balls. Keep in the refrigerator for 30 minutes.

2 Preheat a grill or broiler. Just before grilling the fish balls, take them out of the refrigerator. Push a lemongrass stem through the middle of each one, and with your hand form it into a sausage shape. Then grill the fish "sausages" for about 2 minutes on each side, turning them once.

3 Garnish with cilantro leaves and serve immediately, while still piping hot.

STEAMED FISH WITH SPICED GREEN MANGO

SERVES 4

PREPARATION
about 25 minutes
COOKING
about 20 minutes

Calories per serving *561*
Total fat *41 g (66%)*
Saturated fat *13 g*
Protein *35 g*
Carbohydrate *13 g*
Cholesterol *95 mg*
Vitamins *A, B group, C, E*
Minerals *Potassium, Iron, Zinc, Selenium, Iodine*

Like green papaya, green mango can be treated as a vegetable and lightly cooked. Mackerel has quite a strong aroma and flavor, which will be matched and offset by the spiced mango and coconut. Although the fat content of the dish is high, remember that much of it is in the form of the mackerel's health-giving omega-3 oils.

4 medium-sized mackerel, gutted and cleaned
1 teaspoon coarse sea salt
handful of cilantro leaves, to garnish
2-5 small red bird chilies, cut into thin rounds, to garnish

For the spiced mango:
2 tablespoons peanut or vegetable oil
2 shallots, thinly sliced
2-4 green chilies, seeded and thinly sliced

8 pickled garlic cloves (optional)
1 teaspoon coarsely ground black peppercorns
3 tablespoons desiccated coconut
1 tablespoon nam pla fish sauce
1 teaspoon sugar
½ lime, diced with the peel
2 small green mangoes, peeled and cut into tiny matchsticks
salt

1   Sprinkle the mackerel with the coarse sea salt. Put the fish in a deep plate and steam in a steamer or in a saucepan with an inverted plate at the bottom with water up to the bottom of the upper plate. Steam the fish for 6 minutes. Leave them to cool, remove the skin and bones, and flake the flesh. Set aside.

2   Prepare the spiced mango: in a wok or frying pan, heat the oil and fry the shallots, chilies, and pickled garlic cloves (if you are using them) for 2 minutes, stirring all the time. Add the peppercorns and coconut. Continue to stir for a few minutes, then add the fish sauce, sugar, diced lime, and mangoes. Stir-fry for 2 minutes and adjust the seasoning.

3   Arrange the mango mixture on a platter and spread the fish flakes on top. Sprinkle the garnish over all, and serve immediately at room temperature.

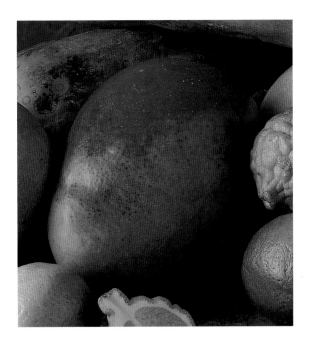

PLA WAN
Caramelized Fish Steaks

Steaks of ocean perch, halibut, cod, or any other firm white fish, or monkfish tails, all respond well to this treatment. Ask your fishmonger for whatever is freshest on the day. Serve with some salad as a first course, or as a main course with rice, accompanied by a cooked vegetable and some chili sauce.

4 fish steaks, weighing about 6 ounces each
juice of ½ lime
1 teaspoon salt

3 tablespoons demerara sugar or brown granulated sugar
2 teaspoons peanut oil

SERVES 4

PREPARATION
about 5 minutes, plus 1 hour's marinating
COOKING
about 5 minutes

1   Rub the pieces of fish all over with the lime juice and then the salt. Leave on a plate for an hour or so.

2   Spread the demerara sugar on a flat plate or tray.

3   When you are ready to cook, grease a nonstick frying pan with the peanut oil and heat it.

4   Coat the fish steaks on both sides with the sugar and carefully arrange them side by side in the pan.

Cook for 2 minutes and turn them over. Continue cooking for another 2 minutes, or longer, depending on the thickness of the fish steaks.

5   Continue heating the sugar that remains in the pan so that it caramelizes a little more, then pour it over all the fish. Serve immediately.

Calories per serving *230*
Total fat *7 g (26%)*
Saturated fat *1 g*
Protein *31 g*
Carbohydrate *12 g*
Cholesterol *78 mg*
Vitamins *B group, E*
Minerals *Potassium, Selenium, Iodine*

KUNG TORD
Marinated and Grilled Shrimp

SERVES 4
as a first course on a salad

PREPARATION
about 25 minutes, plus 30 minutes' to 3 hours' marinating
COOKING
about 4 minutes

Calories per serving *61*
Total fat *3 g (43%)*
Saturated fat *2 g*
Protein *5 g*
Carbohydrate *4 g*
Cholesterol *49 mg*
Vitamins *B group*
Minerals *Potassium, Iron*

16-20 raw jumbo shrimp, shelled and deveined

For the marinade:
1-inch piece of fresh galingale, peeled and finely chopped
1 teaspoon finely chopped lemongrass
4 cilantro roots, chopped

3 shallots, chopped
3 garlic cloves, chopped
2 small fresh or dried chilies, chopped
1 tablespoon chopped creamed coconut
½ cup hot water
juice of 1 small lime
1 teaspoon salt

1 Put all the marinade ingredients in a food processor and blend until smooth. Transfer to a bowl.
2 Butterfly the shrimp: cut each one lengthwise, but leave the halves joined at the tail. Push a wooden toothpick or bamboo skewer through the top halves of the shrimp so that the two halves are held open and flat. Put them in the marinade, coat them well, and leave in a cool place or in the refrigerator for 30 minutes or up to 3 hours. Remove from the refrigerator 30 minutes before you want to cook.
3 Preheat a grill or broiler. Grill the shrimp for 2 minutes on each side, turning once.

YAM TALAY
Cold Salad of Assorted Seafood

SERVES 6-8

PREPARATION
about 20 minutes
COOKING
about 5 minutes, plus cooling and 30 minutes' marinating

Calories per serving *214*
Total fat *6 g (26%)*
Saturated fat *1 g*
Protein *34 g*
Carbohydrate *5 g*
Cholesterol *258 mg*
Vitamins *B group, C, E*
Minerals *Potassium, Iron, Zinc, Selenium, Iodine*

Here in London, I look for a fishmonger with a line of Japanese customers at the door waiting to buy fish for sashimi: that is the place to buy the freshest of seafood for this salad.

1 cooked lobster (see page 80) or 1 pound jumbo shrimp
1 pound baby squid, cut into small bite-sized pieces
½ pound tuna steak
½ pound salmon steak

For the dressing:
4 tablespoons nam pla fish sauce
4 tablespoons lime juice
1 tablespoon superfine sugar
2-3 small red bird chilies, chopped

2 shallots, thinly sliced
1 teaspoon finely chopped lemongrass
2 kaffir lime leaves, finely shredded

For the garnish:
handful of arugula leaves
handful of lamb's lettuce (optional)
½ cucumber, very thinly sliced
2 tablespoons chopped celery leaves
handful of cilantro leaves

Previous pages: Cold Salad of Assorted Seafood, and Marinated and Grilled Shrimp

1   If using jumbo shrimp, poach them for 3 minutes in boiling salted water. When cool enough to handle, shell the lobster or peel the shrimp. Cut the lobster flesh into small bite-sized pieces or slice the shrimp in half lengthwise. Poach the squid pieces similarly for 3 minutes. Poach or broil the fish steaks for 3 minutes. Cut the fish into bite-sized pieces.

2   Mix all the dressing ingredients in a glass salad bowl. Stir to dissolve the sugar. About 30 minutes before serving, mix the seafood into the dressing.

3   To serve, mix the garnish into the seafood in the bowl. Toss well and serve at room temperature.

FISH IN BLACK BEAN SAUCE

My choice of fish here is trout, and because I hate to eat fish with a lot of bones I give here an easy method of filleting them before putting the fish in the sauce. Serve with rice or noodles and some green salad or vegetables.

juice of 1 lime or lemon
1 stalk of lemongrass, cut into 3 pieces
1 teaspoon salt
4 medium-sized trout, each weighing about 9 ounces with the head
handful of basil leaves, to garnish
2 teaspoons fresh green peppercorns, to garnish

For the black bean sauce:
2 tablespoons peanut oil

5 shallots, thinly sliced
2 large green chilies, seeded and thinly sliced
3 scallions, thinly sliced
2 tablespoons canned black bean sauce
2 garlic cloves, chopped
1 teaspoon sugar
1 tablespoon light soy sauce
2 teaspoons lime juice
½ pound button mushrooms, thinly sliced
⅔ cup hot water

SERVES 4

PREPARATION
about 20 minutes, plus cooling
COOKING
about 25 minutes

Calories per serving *254*
Total fat *8 g (29%)*
Saturated fat *None*
Protein *41 g*
Carbohydrate *Low*
Cholesterol *4 g*
Vitamins *B group, C*
Minerals *Potassium, Iron, Zinc, Selenium*

1   Put 4 cups water in a saucepan with the lime or lemon juice, lemongrass, and salt. Bring to a boil and carefully put in the trout. Simmer for 3 minutes, then drain the fish in a colander. Transfer the fish to a flat plate or tray and leave to cool a little. When cool enough to handle, carefully skin the fish, and remove the heads and bones.

2   Make the sauce: heat the oil in a wok or frying pan and fry the shallots, green chilies, and scallions for 3 minutes, stirring often. Remove from heat. Preheat the oven to 320°F.

3   Put the rest of the ingredients for the sauce except the mushrooms in a blender or food processor, adding only 3 tablespoons of the hot water, and blend for a few seconds—do not make this paste too smooth. Reheat the oil with the shallot mixture, stir once, and add the paste. Keep stirring for a few minutes, then add the mushrooms. Stir for 1 minute more, add the remaining hot water, and simmer for 5 minutes. Adjust the seasoning.

4   To finish: arrange the trout side by side on an ovenproof dish, pour the sauce over them, and put in the preheated oven for 8 to 10 minutes. Sprinkle the basil and peppercorns on top just before serving.

HOY MANG PHOU NUENG
Steamed Mussels with Basil

This is instantly recognizable as a Thai dish by its imaginative use of herbs. It strikes just the right balance between the saltiness of the sea and the aromatic tang of cilantro and basil.

SERVES 4
generously as a first course

PREPARATION
about 20 minutes
COOKING
about 20 minutes

Calories per serving *151*
Total fat *3 g (20%)*
Saturated fat *0.5 g*
Protein *21 g*
Carbohydrate *9 g*
Cholesterol *72 mg*
Vitamins *A, B group, E*
Minerals *Potassium, Zinc, Iron, Selenium, Iodine*

4½ pounds mussels, well scrubbed and beards removed
2 stalks of lemongrass, each cut into three pieces
2 red chilies, coarsely chopped
2 tablespoons peanut oil
3 shallots, thinly sliced
2 teaspoons chopped garlic

½-inch piece of fresh ginger, finely chopped
1 tablespoon nam pla fish sauce
1 teaspoon sugar
1 teaspoon crushed black peppercorns
2 tablespoons chopped cilantro leaves, plus more whole leaves for garnish
large handful of basil leaves

1 Scrub and clean the mussels under cold running water. Discard any that are open and don't close on being tapped.

2 Put 7½ cups water in a large saucepan with the lemongrass and chilies and bring to a boil. Add the mussels and cook for 5 minutes. Drain the mussels in a colander and discard any that stay closed. Also discard the lemongrass and chillies.

3 Preheat the oven to 350°F.

4 Heat the oil in a large wok or saucepan and fry the shallots, garlic, and ginger for a minute or two. Add the rest of the ingredients, reserving some of the basil leaves for garnish, and simmer, stirring, for 2 more minutes. Add the mussels and stir well.

5 Lay a large piece of foil on a flat surface and pile the mussels with the shallot mixture in the center. Fold the foil upward and fold over the edges to make a sealed package. Put the package in the oven and cook for 8 minutes.

6 To serve: either transfer equal quantities of mussels and some of the cooking juices to 4 large deep plates, or put everything in a large bowl so that people can help themselves to as much as they want. Garnish with cilantro and basil leaves.

Steamed Mussels with Basil

FISH STEAKS WITH SPICED EGGPLANT

The spiced eggplant referred to here is simply the Hot Eggplant Relish described on page 146. The method used with the fish steaks is to marinate them in tamarind water, shallow-fry them with plenty of shallots in a casserole, and then top them with the relish. In Thailand, the cooking pot is usually earthenware; alternatively, the dish is cooked wrapped in a banana leaf.

SERVES 4

PREPARATION
*about 10 minutes,
plus 1-4 hours'
marinating*
COOKING
about 20 minutes

Calories per serving *264*
Total fat *7 g (25%)*
Saturated fat *1 g*
Protein *34 g*
Carbohydrate *17 g*
Cholesterol *78 mg*
Vitamins *A, B, group, E*
Minerals *Potassium, Iron,
Zinc, Selenium, Iodine*

**4 cod or monkfish steaks, each weighing
about 6 ounces**
4 tablespoons tamarind water (see page 24)
1 teaspoon salt
1 teaspoon sugar
2 tablespoons peanut oil
8 shallots, thinly sliced

2-6 small red bird chilies, thinly sliced
1 tablespoon nam pla fish sauce
4 tablespoons hot water
6 tablespoons Hot Eggplant Relish (page 146)
2 tablespoons chopped mint leaves
1 teaspoon finely chopped lemongrass

1 Put the fish steaks in a glass bowl. Mix the tamarind water with the salt and sugar and pour this over the fish. Turn the steaks over once or twice so that they are well covered in the tamarind mixture. Leave them in the refrigerator for at least 1 hour or up to 4 hours.

2 When you are ready to cook and serve the fish, heat the oil in a frying pan or a casserole and fry the shallots, stirring often, for 5 minutes or until they are just starting to change color. Add the chilies and continue to stir-fry for another minute.

3 Lower the heat and arrange the drained marinated fish in the pan, side by side. Leave to cook for 2 minutes. Turn them over and cook the other sides for another 2 minutes. Add the fish sauce and hot water, and top each fish steak with the eggplant relish (make sure that each steak has an equal amount). Cover the pan and simmer for 3 minutes.

4 Uncover the pan and add the mint leaves and lemongrass. Turn the heat up for 1 minute only. Serve immediately while still very hot, with rice or noodles and vegetables of your choice.

Fish Steaks with Spiced Eggplant

STUFFED CRAB SHELLS

SERVES 4

PREPARATION
about 15 minutes
COOKING
12 minutes

Calories per serving *158*
Total fat *6 g (33%)*
Saturated fat *1 g*
Protein *25 g*
Carbohydrate *1 g*
Cholesterol *131 mg*
Vitamins *B group*
Minerals *Potassium, Iron,
Zinc, Selenium, Iodine*

For this you need small crabs—the shell and the white meat only. Ask your fishmonger for crabs that have not been dressed. This dish makes a good first course, accompanied by Cucumber Relish (page 144).

4 crab shells, cleaned
10 ounces white crabmeat (about 4-5 small crabs)
6 ounces skinless chicken breast fillet, minced
4 garlic cloves, finely chopped

5 cilantro roots, finely chopped, plus 2 tablespoons finely chopped cilantro leaves
2 small dried chilies, crushed in a mortar
1 egg yolk, lightly beaten
1 tablespoon nam pla fish sauce

1 In a bowl, mix all the ingredients except the crab shells. Divide mixture among the shells.

2 Arrange the stuffed crab shells on a flat plate side by side. Pour 2½ cups of water into a saucepan big enough for the plate. Put a trivet or an inverted plate in the saucepan, bring the water to a boil, then put the plate with the crab shells on the trivet or the inverted plate. Cover the saucepan and steam the stuffed shells for 12 minutes.

3 The stuffed shells can be served immediately, or you can put them under the broiler to brown the top of the stuffing a little before serving.

SQUID IN HOT COCONUT SAUCE

SERVES 4

PREPARATION
about 25 minutes
COOKING
about 20 minutes

Calories per serving *635*
Total fat *58 g (82%)*
Saturated fat *12 g*
Protein *23 g*
Carbohydrate *7 g*
Cholesterol *310 mg*
Vitamins *A, B group, C, E*
Minerals *Potassium, Iron,
Zinc, Selenium, Iodine*

1¼ pounds baby squid, each cut into 6 rings
¾ cup hot water
3 tablespoons plain low-fat yogurt
juice of ½ lime
2 tablespoons chopped creamed coconut

For the paste:
2 tablespoons peanut oil
3 shallots, sliced
3 garlic cloves, chopped

2-4 large red chilies, seeded and chopped
2 teaspoons coriander seeds
1 teaspoon cumin seeds
½-inch piece of fresh galingale, peeled and finely chopped
1 teaspoon finely chopped lemongrass
1 teaspoon chopped cilantro roots
1 teaspoon salt
1 teaspoon sugar
2 tablespoons water

1 In a blender or food processor, blend all the ingredients for the paste until smooth. Transfer the paste to a saucepan, heat and stir for 4 minutes, then add the hot water.

2 Bring this sauce almost to a boil and simmer for 8 minutes. Add the yogurt, stirring constantly. Increase the heat until the sauce boils, and add the squid. Cook for 3 minutes. Taste, and add some more salt if necessary. Lastly, add the lime juice and coconut. Stir until the coconut dissolves. Serve hot.

Stuffed Crab Shells served on a bed of mixed salad

LOBSTER IN PIQUANT DRESSING

Naturally, fresh uncooked lobsters are best for this, but in a good fishmonger's or specialty food store you can buy cooked lobsters that are still whole. Don't buy lobsters that are already halved and dressed.

SERVES 4

PREPARATION
about 20 minutes
COOKING
about 5 minutes

Calories per serving *107*
Total fat *2 g (13%)*
Saturated fat *0.3 g*
Protein *21 g*
Carbohydrate *3 g*
Cholesterol *100 mg*
Vitamins *B group, C, E*
Minerals *Potassium, Iron,
Zinc, Selenium, Iodine*

2 medium-sized whole lobsters

For the dressing:
2 tablespoons nam pla fish sauce
juice of ½ lime

2 small red bird chilies, chopped
3 scallions, cut into pieces at an angle
1 tablespoon chopped cilantro leaves
1 teaspoon chopped lemongrass
1 teaspoon sugar

1 Plunge the whole lobsters into lightly salted boiling water in a large saucepan. Uncooked lobsters should be cooked for about 5 minutes. Cooked (red) ones need be heated for 1 minute only to freshen them. Take the lobsters out and let them cool.

2 When they are cool enough to handle, cut the lobsters in half lengthwise with a sharp knife. Discard the inedible parts, namely the head sac, the gills (which look like fingers), and the intestinal vein. Crack the claws, prise out the meat, and put the body and claw meat in the empty head shell.

3 Mix the ingredients for the dressing in a bowl and spoon it on the lobster halves. Serve at room temperature, accompanied by salad.

Lobster in Piquant Dressing

HOT-AND-SOUR SEAFOOD POT

Get your fishmonger to fillet the fish and to give you the heads and bones to make your stock.

SERVES 8-10

PREPARATION
about 40 minutes
COOKING
about 1 hour

Calories per serving *268*
Total fat *10 g (34%)*
Saturated fat *3 g*
Protein *38 g*
Carbohydrate *6 g*
Cholesterol *144 mg*
Vitamins *A, B, Group, C,*
E
Minerals *Calcium,*
Potassium, Iron, Zinc,
Selenium, Iodine

1 pound mussels or cockles, cleaned, discarding any
that stay open when tapped
1 whole turbot or 2 whole mahimahi, about
2¼ pounds
1 pound each filleted monkfish tails, cod and
salmon
1 pound raw jumbo shrimp, shelled and deveined
1 tablespoon peanut oil
3 shallots, thinly sliced
2 red chilies, seeded and sliced
1 pound straw or button mushrooms, quartered
1 pound Chinese cabbage, coarsely chopped
large handful of celery leaves, coarsely chopped

1 cup hot water
2 tablespoons chopped creamed coconut
juice of 1 lime, or 3 tablespoons tamarind water

For the stock:
2 quantities Basic Thai Vegetable Stock (page 44)
3 kaffir lime leaves
2 red chilies, sliced
10 ripe tomatoes, skinned, seeded, and chopped
2 teaspoons ginger juice (see page 21)
juice of 2 limes
pepper
2 tablespoons chopped cilantro leaves

1 Make the stock: put the fish trimmings, but not the shrimp shells, in a very large pot. Add cold water to cover and the Basic Vegetable Stock ingredients with the lime leaves and chilies. Bring to the boil and simmer for 30 minutes, skimming the froth.

2 Meanwhile, half fill another pan with water. Add about ½ teaspoon of salt and bring to the boil. Add the mussels or cockles, cover, and simmer for 4 minutes. With a slotted spoon, transfer the mussels or cockles to a colander. Discard any that stay closed.

3 Strain the stock through a cheesecloth-lined colander into another large pan or heatproof casserole. Heat this clear stock and add to it the remaining stock ingredients. Simmer for 5 minutes, and adjust the seasoning. Up to this point everything can be prepared up to 24 hours in advance, allowed to cool, and stored in the refrigerator.

4 When ready to serve, bring the stock back to

boiling point. Lower the heat and carefully add the fish and shrimp. Simmer for 3 minutes and add the mussels or cockles. Remove from the heat and cover.

5 In a smaller saucepan, heat the oil. When hot, add the shallots and chilies, stir-fry for 2 minutes, then add the mushrooms. Continue to stir-fry for another minute, then add the rest of the ingredients. Bring back to the boil, then simmer for 3 minutes.

6 To serve the soup: transfer most of the stock to a smaller pan. Keep at a simmer. Put one or two pieces of each fish into individual soup bowls, and ladle stock over each. Serve immediately. (Do not reheat the fish and shellfish.)

7 To serve the main course: if you cooked the fish and shellfish in a pan, not a casserole, transfer them to a serving dish with the remaining stock. Pour the hot vegetables with the sauce over the fish. Serve with plain steamed rice and a bowl of chili sauce.

Hot-and-sour Seafood Pot

Poultry

I used to think that Southeast Asia would be the last home of the truly free-range, jaywalking chicken. It is true that on country roads you still need to drive carefully to avoid them, and in country markets even today you can buy small, athletic birds that take a lot of cooking to get them anywhere near tender. Things are changing, though. On a recent journey, after we had driven many miles in silence, I remarked for the sake of saying something, "Oh look, there's a rice mill!" Our driver, not missing a beat, pointed out of the opposite window and said, "Look, there's a chicken mill!" And, indeed, there were the long timber sheds, filled no doubt with battery hens. Is this progress, I wonder? At least I suppose mass-produced poultry brings yesterday's luxury food down to a price that everyone in the new Asia can afford.

Leaving aside this moral dilemma, there are a great number of delicious Thai recipes for cooking chickens and ducks. I have concentrated here on chickens, because they have far less fat on them than any water-based bird could get away with. However, I couldn't resist including the Braised Duck with Squash and Mushrooms, which being without any skin is as healthy and low in fat as a duck dish can well be, and a particular favorite in my own household.

The dishes in this section are all wonderfully aromatic, and I have especially tried to select recipes that will make supermarket chicken breasts feel tender and moist in the mouth; so often they become dry and fibrous when cooked, especially if they have been frozen.

Stuffed Breast of Chicken with Red Curry Sauce (page 86)

STUFFED BREAST OF CHICKEN WITH RED CURRY SAUCE

It is a tradition in Thailand and in neighboring states—Laos, Vietnam, Cambodia—that ducks and chickens are stuffed, whole, with a long list of aromatic ingredients, including glutinous or sweet rice. Often the rice for stuffing is colored green. Here, by using only the breast meat without the skin, I have considerably cut the cooking time. Using asparagus alone as the stuffing greatly reduces the fat and calories, and it looks and tastes delicious. (See previous page.)

SERVES 4

PREPARATION
about 15 minutes
COOKING
about 40 minutes

Calories per serving *212*
Total fat *5 g (21%)*
Saturated fat *1 g*
Protein *36 g*
Carbohydrate *7 g*
Cholesterol *92 mg*
Vitamins *A, B group, C, E*
Minerals *Calcium,*
Potassium, Iron, Zinc,
Selenium, Iodine

2 whole boneless skinless chicken breasts
1 teaspoon nam pla fish sauce
large pinch of chili powder
1 teaspoon sugar
1 tablespoon lime juice
16 asparagus stalks, trimmed

For the red curry sauce:
8 tablespoons Red Curry Paste (page 116)
2 cups hot water
3 tablespoons low-fat yogurt
handful of basil leaves, plus more for garnish
scallion, sliced at an angle, to garnish (optional)
red chili, seeded and sliced, to garnish (optional)

1 Flatten the chicken breasts with a rolling pin, and cut each one, following the grain, into 4 thin strips. Put these strips in a glass bowl. Mix the fish sauce, chili powder, sugar, and lime juice. Rub the chicken strips well with this mixture and set aside in a cool place.

2 Boil some water in a saucepan, and add a large pinch of salt. Add the asparagus and cook for 2 minutes. Drain the asparagus in a colander and refresh under cold running water.

3 Make the sauce: put the curry paste in a saucepan and simmer, stirring often, for 3 minutes. Add the hot water, and continue to simmer for 20 minutes, stirring occasionally. Add the yogurt a spoonful at a time, stirring continuously, until all of it is incorporated in the sauce. Continue to simmer gently for 10 minutes.

4 While the sauce is cooking, heat 5 cups of water in another saucepan.

5 On a flat surface, lay 4 strips of chicken meat side by side, overlapping a little. Lay 4 asparagus stalks across the strips. Then roll the chicken strips tightly around the asparagus. (The stalks remain straight.) Wrap the roll with plastic wrap, securing both ends with a twist. Repeat with the remaining chicken and asparagus.

6 Plunge these rolls into the water as it boils. Lower the heat, cover the pan, and cook for 6 minutes. Discard the water, unwrap the chicken rolls, and put them side by side on a tray. Leave them to cool.

7 Adjust the seasoning of the sauce. When the stuffed chicken is cool enough to handle, slice each roll into 4 to 6 pieces and carefully put the slices in the sauce. Simmer for 5 minutes more, add the basil leaves, and serve hot, garnished with more basil leaves and chopped scallion and chili if you wish. Plain boiled jasmine rice and either cooked vegetables or a salad make good accompaniments.

HOT GINGER CHICKEN WITH RICE NOODLES

2 whole chicken breasts, on the bone
1 teaspoon salt
2 ounces ginger, peeled and very thinly sliced
4 scallions
1 large green chili, seeded
1 tablespoon light soy sauce
2 teaspoons lemon juice
½ teaspoon sugar
8 ounces rice noodles

For the sauce:
1 teaspoon nam pla fish sauce
3 scallions, thinly sliced
1 large red chili, seeded and thinly sliced
2 ounces snow peas or sugar peas, sliced into tiny strips
handful of cilantro leaves

SERVES 4

PREPARATION
about 20 minutes
COOKING
about 50 minutes

Calories per serving *365*
Total fat *2 g (4%)*
Saturated fat *0.5 g*
Protein *36 g*
Carbohydrate *50 g*
Cholesterol *91 mg*
Vitamins *B group, C*
Minerals *Potassium, Iron, Zinc, Selenium, Iodine*

1 Put the chicken breasts in a saucepan and add 5 cups cold water and the salt. Bring to a boil, reduce the heat, and simmer for 10 minutes. Remove the chicken breasts with a slotted spoon and place on a plate. When cool enough to handle, skin and bone them. Put the bones and skins back into the saucepan and continue to simmer until the stock has reduced by half, about 10 minutes. Remove from the heat. If you prefer, skim off the fat.

2 Have ready a large piece of foil. Cut each chicken-breast half into 4 slices. Arrange side by side on the foil.

3 Cut the thin slices of ginger into tiny strips. Do the same with the scallions and green chilies, and divide them equally among the chicken slices.

4 In a small bowl, mix the soy sauce, lemon juice, and sugar. Stir to dissolve the sugar, then pour over the chicken slices. Now fold the foil over and fold its edges together to make a package. Up to this point everything can be prepared in advance.

5 Preheat the oven to 320°F. Put the noodles in a large bowl and cover with boiling water. Leave to soak for 15 minutes. Drain and keep warm.

6 Heat the foil package in the oven for 15 minutes.

7 Meanwhile, heat the stock in the pan and simmer gently. Add the other ingredients for the sauce about 2 minutes before serving.

8 To serve: use the largest, deepest soup plates that you have. Divide the noodles among them and pile them in each bowl, a little to one side. Take the chicken out of the oven, unwrap, and arrange each breast half next to the noodles. Divide the cooking juices among them. Serve the sauce separately in a bowl or a sauceboat.

BOILED CHICKEN BREAST WITH THAI DRESSING AND RED PEPPERS

For this simple chicken dish, Thai cooks would shred the boiled chicken by hand, and cut the boiled pepper into strips. The dressing is made very hot and sweet-and-sour, with loads of lemongrass and cilantro leaves. Here is my version, not exactly westernized, but I know that roasted peppers taste better than boiled ones.

SERVES 4

PREPARATION
about 20 minutes
COOKING
*about 30 minutes,
plus cooling*

Calories per serving *189*
Total fat *3 g (14%)*
Saturated fat *1 g*
Protein *32 g*
Carbohydrate *8 g*
Cholesterol *91 mg*
Vitamins *A, B group, C*
Minerals *Potassium, Iron,
Zinc, Selenium, Iodine*

2 whole skinless boneless chicken breasts
½ teaspoon salt
2 red bell peppers, rubbed with a little olive oil

For the dressing:
2 teaspoons finely chopped lemongrass
2-4 small red bird chilies, finely chopped

juice of 1 lime
1-2 teaspoons sugar
2 tablespoons nam pla fish sauce
½-inch piece of fresh galingale, finely chopped (optional)
2 tablespoons chopped cilantro leaves
salt (optional)

1 Preheat the oven to 350°F. Heat 5 cups of water in a saucepan and, when boiling, put in the chicken breasts and the salt. Lower the heat a little and cook the chicken for 8 minutes. Remove from heat and leave the chicken breasts to cool in the water.

2 Put the peppers in a roasting pan, place in the preheated oven, and roast for 25 to 30 minutes. Take them out and leave them to cool a little. When they are cool enough to handle, peel and seed the peppers, but make sure that you do this over a bowl. Strain the juice that comes out of the peppers through a sieve into another bowl, and save this juice to be

mixed with the dressing.

3 Shred the chicken meat, or slice it into nice thin slices. The peppers can also be cut into thin strips, or into diamond shapes if you prefer.

4 Mix the ingredients for the dressing in a bowl, adding the reserved juices from the peppers. Just before serving, put the chicken slices and bell peppers in the bowl with the dressing. Toss to mix well. Taste, and add some salt if necessary. Serve at room temperature on a bed of mixed leaves and herbs or on hot plain boiled rice noodles.

Boiled Chicken Breast with Thai Dressing and Red Peppers

PAD KAI KAPROW
Braised Chicken with Green Peppercorns and Basil

*Green peppercorns and basil are very often used in combination as a flavoring for meat dishes. In this recipe
I have substituted fresh basil leaves for the garnish of crisp deep-fried basil that would be used in Thailand.*

SERVES 4

PREPARATION
about 15 minutes
COOKING
about 10 minutes

Calories per serving *190*
Total fat *4 g (21%)*
Saturated fat *1 g*
Protein *32 g*
Carbohydrate *6 g*
Cholesterol *91 mg*
Vitamins *A, B group, C*
Minerals *Potassium, Iron,
Zinc, Selenium, Iodine*

2 whole skinless chicken breasts
1 tablespoon vegetable oil
3 shallots, thinly sliced
2 garlic cloves, thinly sliced
1-3 small red bird chilies, thinly sliced
2 tablespoons nam pla fish sauce

4 tablespoons hot water
2 teaspoons fresh green peppercorns
juice of ½ lime
1 teaspoon sugar (optional)
handful or more of basil leaves
salt and pepper

1 Cut the chicken into julienne strips. Heat the oil in a nonstick saucepan, add the shallots and garlic, and stir-fry for 2 minutes. Add the chilies, fish sauce, and chicken. Stir constantly for 2 minutes, then add the hot water. Reduce the heat and cover. Simmer for 5 to 6 minutes.

2 Uncover the pan and add the peppercorns, lime juice, and sugar (if using). Stir for 30 seconds, then add the basil leaves. Stir again, taste, and add salt and pepper if necessary.

3 Serve hot, with boiled rice or rice noodles.

Braised Chicken with Green Peppercorns and Basil

JULIENNE OF CHICKEN BREAST WITH CRISP-FRIED BASIL AND CELERY ROOT

If you think this dish is good to look at, I can assure you it tastes as good as it looks. The green and red chilies are not here just for color: they give you vitamins A and C along with their own delicious mouth-warming heat. The hotness will not overpower you, because you will only taste the chilies in tiny slices.

If necessary, the dish may be made without deep-frying the garnish; simply blanch the celery root until just tender but still crunchy, and use the basil leaves as they are.

SERVES 4

PREPARATION
*about 25 minutes,
plus 30 minutes'
marinating*
COOKING
about 15 minutes

Calories per serving *229*
Total fat *7 g (29%)*
Saturated fat *2 g*
Protein *33 g*
Carbohydrate *8 g*
Cholesterol *91 mg*
Vitamins *A, B group, C, E*
Minerals *Potassium, Iron,
Zinc, Selenium, Iodine*

2 whole skinless chicken breasts, cut into thin julienne strips
peanut oil for frying
6 ounces peeled celery root, sliced thinly, then cut into tiny sticks
handful of basil leaves
3 shallots, thinly sliced
3 green chilies, seeded and thinly sliced
3 tablespoons hot water (optional)
salt and pepper

For the marinade:
2 tablespoons nam pla fish sauce or light soy sauce
1 tablespoon lime juice
1 teaspoon tiny strips of lime or kaffir lime peel
3 red chilies, seeded and thinly sliced at an angle
2 garlic cloves, crushed
2 teaspoons finely chopped lemongrass
2 tablespoons finely chopped scallions
1 teaspoon demerara or brown granulated sugar (optional)

1 Put all the ingredients for the marinade in a glass bowl, and marinate the chicken slices in it for 30 minutes. Meanwhile, prepare the other ingredients.

2 If deep-frying the garnish: heat about ½ cup of peanut oil, preferably in a wok, and fry the celery root sticks until they are light brown. Take them out, drain them on a plate lined with paper towels, and set aside. Reheat the oil and fry the basil leaves for about 2 minutes, stirring all the time. Remove and drain them on paper towels. They will become crisp when they cool. Pour most of the oil from the wok into a small bowl, but leave about 2 tablespoonfuls in the wok.

3 Reheat the oil in the wok, or add about 2 tablespoons if you have not been deep-frying, and fry the

shallots for 2 minutes, stirring continuously. Add the chicken pieces and the marinade, and stir-fry for 2 minutes. Lower the heat, cover the wok, and let the chicken cook in the steam for 2 to 3 minutes.

4 Uncover the wok and stir the chicken pieces briskly to unstick them from the wok or pan. Add up to 3 tablespoons of hot water if necessary. Add the green chilies and continue stir-frying for another 2 minutes. Season with salt and pepper, stir again, and taste. Adjust the seasoning if necessary.

5 Divide the chicken among 4 warmed serving plates, piling the pieces in the center of each. Put the celery root on top of the chicken, and spread the basil leaves over all. Serve immediately, with green vegetables and rice.

Julienne of Chicken Breast with Crisp-fried Basil and Celery Root

BAKED CHICKEN WITH PICKLED ONIONS

This is an adaptation of a northern Thai dish, traditionally cooked in coconut milk. Baking it without coconut milk makes the pickled onions taste more piquant, though here I use much less chili than a Thai cook normally would. I also use the chicken skins to start the cooking, so no oil is needed.

SERVES 4

PREPARATION
about 15 minutes
COOKING
about 1 hour

Calories per serving *142*
Total fat *2 g (11%)*
Saturated fat *0.4 g*
Protein *22 g*
Carbohydrate *10 g*
Cholesterol *70 mg*
Vitamins *B group, C*
Minerals *Potassium, Iron, Zinc, Selenium, Iodine*

1 whole boneless breast and 2 boneless legs of chicken
6 garlic cloves, finely sliced
1 teaspoon ground white pepper
2 teaspoons salt
4 tablespoons hot water
20 pearl onions or small red Asian onions

juice of 1 or 2 limes
2-4 small red bird chilies, chopped
1-2 teaspoons sugar
1 tablespoon nam pla fish sauce
2 tablespoons chopped scallions, green part only
4 tablespoons chopped cilantro leaves

1 Preheat the oven to 325°F.

2 Skin the chicken pieces and cut the meat into ½-inch cubes. Coarsely chop the skin and put it in a saucepan. Stir-fry the skin until it becomes oily, then add the meat and garlic and stir-fry for 3 minutes. Take out the skins and discard, then add the ground pepper, 1 teaspoon of the salt, and the hot water to the meat and garlic in the pan. Stir again once and simmer for 2 more minutes, then transfer the mixture to an ovenproof dish with a lid.

3 In another saucepan, heat the pearl onions or small red onions together with the lime juice, chilies, remaining salt, the sugar, and 4 tablespoons water.

Simmer until all the juice has evaporated and the onions have caramelized, about 5 minutes.

4 Add the caramelized onions to the chicken in the ovenproof dish. Add the fish sauce, and stir so that the ingredients are well mixed. Put the lid on, and bake in the oven for 35 to 40 minutes.

5 Take the dish out of the oven, uncover, and adjust the seasoning. Add the scallions and cilantro leaves. Put the cover back, return the dish to the oven, and leave it there for 2 minutes. Serve immediately, while piping hot, with plain steamed glutinous rice or other white rice.

EGG NOODLES WITH CHICKEN AND BAMBOO SHOOTS

Chicken breast meat and bamboo shoots make a characteristic Thai combination of ingredients to go with noodles. In fact, this is the most basic and the simplest of all noodle dishes. Furthermore, you can make it into either fried noodles or noodle soup.

8 ounces egg noodles
1 teaspoon salt
2 tablespoons peanut oil or vegetable oil
3 shallots, thinly sliced
2 garlic cloves, thinly sliced
2-inch piece of fresh ginger, finely chopped
1-2 large red chilies, seeded and thinly sliced
½ chicken breast, sliced into small bite-sized pieces
4 ounces canned sliced bamboo shoots, drained and rinsed in cold water

4 ounces white cabbage leaves, coarsely shredded
2 tomatoes, skinned, seeded, and chopped
2 tablespoons chopped scallions
handful of cilantro leaves
1 tablespoon nam pla fish sauce
1 tablespoon light soy sauce
4 tablespoons chicken stock (for fried noodles)
or 5 cups chicken stock (for noodle soup)

Serves 4
as a one-dish meal

Preparation
about 25 minutes
Cooking
about 15 minutes
plus cooling the noodles

Calories per serving *349*
Total fat *11 g (28%)*
Saturated fat *3 g*
Protein *17 g*
Carbohydrate *48 g*
Cholesterol *40 mg*
Vitamins *A, B group, C, E*
Minerals *Potassium, Iron, Zinc*

1 To cook the noodles: boil 7½ cups water in a large pan with the salt. Add the noodles, increase the heat, and push them down with a wooden spoon. Try to loosen the bundle of noodles by moving them around in the boiling water. Boil them for 3 minutes, then pour the noodles into a colander and run cold water over them, turning them over and over by hand until they are cool. Leave them to drain.

2 Heat the oil in a wok or large saucepan, and stir-fry the shallots, garlic, ginger, and chilies for 2 minutes. Add the chicken, bamboo shoots, and cabbage. Continue to stir-fry for 2 more minutes, then add the rest of the ingredients, except the stock. Stir-fry again for 2 minutes and serve with noodles.

3 To make fried noodles: when you are ready to serve, add 4 tablespoons of chicken stock to the wok or pan. Increase the heat and add the noodles. Stir the noodles to mix them well with the chicken and vegetables. Taste, and add more salt, fish sauce, or soy sauce as necessary. Serve hot.

4 To make noodle soup: when ready to serve, add 5 cups of chicken stock to the chicken and vegetable mixture. Bring to a boil and add the noodles. Stir for 1 minute and serve hot.

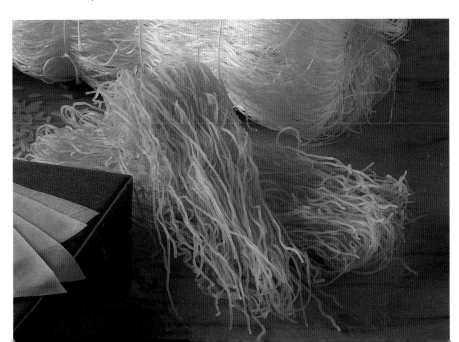

BRAISED DUCK WITH SQUASH AND MUSHROOMS

Of the many varieties of squash to be found in Thailand, the most common are pumpkins—usually small, with dark green or yellow-orange skins—and winter melons. These are usually available in Asian markets in the West. If you can't find them, butternut squash or yellow zucchini from the supermarket will do very well.

The Thais use fresh straw mushrooms for this dish. I suggest, instead, fresh porcini (cèpes), when in season, chestnut mushrooms, or fresh or dried shiitakes. If you use dried shiitakes, first rinse them well and then soak them for 20 minutes in water which has just boiled. This soaking water can then be used in place of chicken stock.

SERVES 4

PREPARATION
*about 15 minutes,
plus at least 1 hour's
marinating*
COOKING
about 20 minutes

Calories per serving *262*
Total fat *14 g (49%)*
Saturated fat *4 g*
Protein *29 g*
Carbohydrate *5 g*
Cholesterol *143 mg*
Vitamins *B group, C, E*
Minerals *Potassium, Iron,
Zinc*

2 whole skinless duck breasts
3 tablespoons dark soy sauce
1 teaspoon freshly ground black pepper
1 tablespoon lime juice
½ kaffir lime or unwaxed lime
2 tablespoons peanut oil or vegetable oil
3 shallots, thinly sliced
2 garlic cloves, thinly sliced

2½ cups chicken stock (optional)
*6 ounces peeled squash or unpeeled zucchini, cut
into large dice*
*4 ounces fresh mushrooms, quartered,
or 2 ounces dried shiitake mushrooms, soaked,
stems removed, and quartered*
1 tablespoon nam pla fish sauce
cilantro leaves, to garnish

1 Cut each duck breast half diagonally into 6 slices. Put the slices in a glass bowl and add the soy sauce, pepper, and lime juice. Mix well and refrigerate for at least 1 hour or up to 24 hours.

2 Chop the kaffir lime or lime into small dice, discarding all the seeds.

3 Heat the oil in a wok or frying pan and add the duck slices. Stir-fry them for 2 minutes. Add the shallots and garlic and stir-fry for 1 or 2 minutes

more. Add the stock or the mushroom soaking water and bring to a boil. Cook for 10 minutes.

4 Stir in the squash or zucchini and the mushrooms. Lower the heat, cover the pan, and continue cooking for 5 minutes.

5 Uncover the pan, turn up the heat, and add the chopped lime and the fish sauce. Stir for a minute or so. Adjust the seasoning and serve hot, garnished with cilantro leaves and with plenty of boiled rice.

Braised Duck with Squash and Mushrooms

Rice & Noodles

Rice is the staple food in Thailand, and rice noodles come second. The Thai words used when people invite guests to dinner actually mean "come and have rice with us." Egg noodles, which are considered to be Chinese, are also very popular.

I strongly recommend that we should follow the Thai example and always use the best rice we can get. Thailand is the world's biggest exporter of rice, growing and trading many different grades and varieties, all with subtly different textures and flavors. Thai jasmine rice of the highest grade is exported to countries that can afford to pay for it. Cheaper varieties go to neighboring countries, while those countries export their best rice to earn foreign currency.

Jasmine rice is sometimes described as "fragrant," "scented" or "perfumed," simply because it smells so good when it is cooking. When perfectly cooked, the grains are slightly sticky, which is how everyone in Southeast Asia likes their rice to be. So-called sticky or glutinous rice is a different variety of rice that is much more sticky and needs longer cooking: the Thais use it mainly for sweets and cakes, though it is the staple of people in northern Thailand and across the border in Laos. The difference between sticky and non-sticky rice comes simply from the different proportions of two different types of starch in the grains.

Fried Rice with Pineapple (page 101)

COOKING RICE

First measure the rice using a cup. Wash the rice in cold water: put it in the pan, pour enough water over it to cover it, swirl it around with your fingers, and pour the water away. Repeat this process once or twice if you like. The last time, pour away as much of the water as you easily can—there is no need to squeeze out every last drop. Then measure the water for cooking in the same cup as you used to measure the rice. For 2 cups of rice, use 2 cups of water. An extra ¼ or ½ cup of water will make the rice a little softer. If, after washing, you drain the rice very thoroughly in a sieve or colander, then when you put it in the pan add that extra ¼ cup or ½ cup. However, don't add extra water if you are going to fry the rice afterward—rice for frying needs to be dry and not too soft.

To cook rice in an ordinary saucepan, put the rice and the right quantity of water into the pan and bring the water to a boil (don't put in any salt). Stir once with a wooden spoon, and let the rice bubble very gently, uncovered, until all the water has been absorbed. Then, after stirring the rice once more with a wooden spoon, finish cooking in one of the four following ways:

1   Keep the rice in the same saucepan and cover it tightly. Turn the heat as low as possible, and leave the rice undisturbed for 12 minutes. Then take the saucepan from the heat and put it on top of a wet cloth (this is important to prevent the bottom layer from sticking to the pan). After 3 minutes, uncover the pan and transfer the rice to a serving bowl. Serve it hot, or leave it to cool if you are going to make fried rice.

2   Transfer the rice from the saucepan to a steamer, and steam for 12 minutes.

3   Transfer the rice from the saucepan to an ovenproof dish with a lid, and cook in the oven, covered, for 12 minutes at 350°F.

4   Transfer the rice from the saucepan to a microwavable container. Cover with a plate or waxed paper and microwave on full power for 4 to 5 minutes.

The easiest way of all is to use an electric rice cooker, which guarantees perfect results almost without trying. Put the washed rice in the cooker with the right amount of water. Put the lid on and switch to the "cook" setting. When the rice is cooked, the cooker will automatically switch to "warm." You can leave the rice in the cooker to keep it warm for a few minutes before you are ready to start the meal. I suggest, though, that you turn the cooker off completely as soon as the rice is cooked to prevent it from getting too dry, especially at the bottom.

FRIED RICE WITH EGGS

SERVES 4

PREPARATION
*about 15 minutes,
plus boiling and
cooling the rice*
COOKING
about 10 minutes

This is the Thai version of the simplest kind of fried rice, the way most people in Asia like it for breakfast. Accompanied by satay *or broiled fish and a good crunchy salad, it becomes a light but satisfying lunch or supper.*

2 tablespoons vegetable oil	*2 eggs, lightly beaten*
2 shallots, thinly sliced	*3 cups cold plain boiled rice*
1 garlic clove, finely chopped	*3 tablespoons chopped scallions*
1 large red chili, seeded and finely chopped	*salt and pepper*

1 Heat the oil in a wok and stir-fry the shallots, garlic, and chili for 2 minutes.

2 Add the eggs, stirring to scramble them. Add the rice, and toss and stir it for 2 minutes. Mix in the scallions and cook, stirring frequently, for 2 more minutes. Taste and adjust the seasoning. Serve hot.

Calories per serving *222*
Total fat *10 g (40%)*
Saturated fat *2 g*
Protein *7 g*
Carbohydrate *28 g*
Cholesterol *116 mg*
Vitamins *B group, C, E*
Minerals *Potassium, Iron, Zinc, Iodine*

KHAO PHAD SAPPAROT
Fried Rice with Pineapple

I suggest you serve this as a one-dish meal, with other fresh fruit to follow. (See page 99.)

4 small or 2 medium-sized pineapples
salt and pepper
2 tablespoons peanut oil
2 shallots, thinly sliced
1 garlic clove, finely chopped
2 large red chilies, seeded and finely chopped
2 eggs, lightly beaten (optional)
3 cups cold plain boiled rice

1 tablespoon tomato paste
½-inch piece of fresh ginger, finely chopped
2 tablespoons chopped scallions plus a few more
scallions, sliced at an angle, to garnish
2 tablespoons chopped cilantro leaves
2 tablespoons nam pla fish sauce
12 raw jumbo shrimp, shelled and deveined
2 large red tomatoes, peeled and quartered

Serves 4

Preparation
about 45 minutes, plus boiling and cooling the rice, and 20 minutes' salting
Cooking
about 15 minutes

Calories per serving *317*
Total fat *11 g (30%)*
Saturated fat *2 g*
Protein *11 g*
Carbohydrate *47 g*
Cholesterol *145 mg*
Vitamins *A, B group, C, E*
Minerals *Calcium, Potassium, Iron, Zinc, Iodine*

1 If using small pineapples, cut each across the top, about 2 inches below the base of the leaves. With a sharp pointed knife, carefully separate the flesh from the skin, leaving a wall of flesh about ¾ inch thick. Cut larger pineapples in half lengthwise, leaving the stiff pointed leaves as decoration. Then remove the cores and cut out the flesh, leaving a similar wall about ¾ inch thick.

2 Sprinkle the insides of the pineapples with salt and set aside for 20 minutes. Then rinse the salt away under cold running water. Pat them dry, inside and out, with a cloth or paper towels, and set aside to be filled with the fried rice when you are ready to serve.

3 Discard the pineapple cores. Dice the flesh – not too small or it will break up in cooking. Place half of the diced pineapple in a bowl, sprinkled with a little salt. Use the remainder for another recipe.

4 Heat half the oil in a wok and stir-fry the shallots, garlic, and chilies for 2 minutes. If you are using eggs, add them now, stirring to scramble them. Add the rice. Toss and stir it for 2 minutes. Add the tomato paste and stir, mixing it well with the rice. Taste, and adjust the seasoning. Remove from the heat while you cook the shrimp.

5 In another wok or frying pan, heat the remaining oil and stir-fry the ginger, scallions, and cilantro for a minute. Add the fish sauce and shrimp. Cook for 2 minutes, stirring occasionally. Add the tomatoes and diced pineapple, then adjust the seasoning.

6 Give it one good stir, then transfer the entire mixture to the wok with the fried rice. Heat gently, stirring carefully, for 1 to 2 minutes. Divide the fried rice among the hollowed-out pineapples and serve immediately, garnished with sliced scallions.

GLUTINOUS RICE STUFFED WITH SHRIMP AND COCONUT

People in the north of Thailand, like their neighbors in Laos, have a preference for glutinous rice or sticky rice. The rice is steamed and served from a woven bamboo basket. You pick up the rice with the fingers of your right hand and then dip it into, or fill it with, whatever you fancy from the side dishes in front of you. In Chiang Mai, street food vendors will sell you packets of glutinous rice, either by itself or with a savory filling such as shrimp and coconut. They cook it in thin segments of green bamboo. This is how I make and serve it.

SERVES 4-6

PREPARATION
*about 20 minutes,
plus 2 hours' soaking*
COOKING
about 20 minutes

Calories per serving *389*
Total fat *8 g (17%)*
Saturated fat *3 g*
Protein *20 g*
Carbohydrate *58 g*
Cholesterol *146 mg*
Vitamins *B group, E*
Minerals *Calcium,
Potassium, Iron, Zinc,
Selenium, Iodine*

*1 pound glutinous rice, soaked in cold water
for 2 hours
2 tablespoons vegetable oil
2 shallots, thinly sliced
1 large red chili, seeded and finely chopped
4 ounces leeks, thinly sliced
1 teaspoon finely choppedlemon grass*

*2 kaffir lime leaves, finely shredded
1 pound small cooked peeled shrimp, coarsely
chopped
2 tablespoons freshly grated or desiccated (dried,
unsweetened) coconut
salt and pepper
cilantro leaves, to garnish*

1 Cook the rice while you are making the filling. Drain the rice and then steam it in a rice steamer or double saucepan for 20 minutes.

2 Meanwhile, make the filling: heat the oil in a wok or frying pan and stir-fry the shallots, chili, and leeks for 2 minutes. Add the lemongrass, kaffir lime leaves, and shrimp. Continue stirring for 2 more minutes. Add the coconut, with 2 tablespoonfuls of water if you are using desiccated coconut. Stir and season with salt and pepper. Take the pan off the heat and cover it to keep it warm.

3 To serve: transfer the rice and the filling to separate plates, and invite your guests to help themselves to both. They can roll their own rice and spread the filling themselves.

4 Alternatively, divide the rice into 24 equal portions, and do the same with the filling. Put one portion of rice on an 8-inch square of plastic wrap or foil. Warm a tablespoon in a glass of hot water and flatten the rice with the back of the wet spoon. Put the spoon back in the water. Using a different spoon, spread a portion of the filling on the rice. Using the wrap or foil, roll the rice around the filling into a log shape like a croquette. Unwrap it. Repeat until you have 24 filled rice rolls. Serve warm or cold.

5 If you want to serve the rice rolls hot, steam them for 3 minutes or put them all on a plate and microwave them for 2 minutes on high. Serve garnished with cilantro leaves.

Glutinous Rice Stuffed with Shrimp and Coconut

VEGETARIAN RICE NOODLES

Traditionally, this dish is made with fresh noodles. The Thais called them longxu *noodles. You may sometimes be able to buy them in a Thai food shop. Alternatively, use the same noodles as for the Rice Noodles with Fish Curry on page 110. In addition to the vegetables and sauce described here, another good dish to accompany these noodles is Tofu in Yellow Bean Sauce (page 138).*

8 ounces rice noodles (rice vermicelli)
5 cups hot water
8 ounces yard-long beans or green beans, cut into 1-inch pieces
8 ounces cauliflower or broccoli florets
8 ounces bean sprouts

For the sauce:
2 tablespoons vegetable oil
4 shallots, thinly sliced
3 garlic cloves, thinly sliced

2 ounces split red lentils, or mung beans soaked in cold water for 30 minutes and then drained
2 tablespoons Red Curry Paste (page 116)
2 tablespoons chopped creamed coconut
juice of 1 lime
salt and pepper

For the garnish:
2 tablespoons crisp-fried shallots (see page 149)
2 tablespoons crushed dried large red chilies, briefly dry-fried

SERVES 4-6

PREPARATION
about 20 minutes, plus 30 minutes' soaking
COOKING
about 20 minutes

Calories per serving *285*
Total fat *9 g (28%)*
Saturated fat *4 g*
Protein *8 g*
Carbohydrate *42 g*
Cholesterol *None*
Vitamins *A, B1, B3, B6, Folate, C, E*
Minerals *Potassium, Iron, Zinc*

1 Put the rice noodles in a large bowl or saucepan and pour the hot water over them to cover. Cover the bowl or pan and leave the noodles undisturbed for 15 minutes. Drain them, and arrange in clusters on a large serving plate.

2 While the noodles are soaking, make the sauce: heat the oil in a saucepan and stir-fry the shallots and garlic for 2 minutes. Add the split mung beans or red lentils and the curry paste. Stir for another minute and add 2½ cups water. Bring to a boil and add the chopped creamed coconut and lime juice.

Simmer, uncovered, for 10 minutes. Adjust the seasoning and set aside.

3 Boil the vegetables separately: the yard-long or green beans for 4 minutes, the cauliflower or broccoli for 3 minutes, and 1 minute for the bean sprouts. Arrange side by side on the serving platter.

4 If necessary, re-heat the sauce and transfer to a bowl. Serve everything immediately, with the garnishes in separate small bowls, asking your guests to help themselves.

Vegetarian Rice Noodles

FRIED RICE WITH SEAFOOD

Good fried rice should not be oily. One way to achieve this is to fry the rice and the seafood separately, and only mix them just before serving. Better still, simply put the seafood on top of the fried rice as a garnish.

SERVES 4

PREPARATION
*about 35 minutes,
plus boiling and
cooling the rice*
COOKING
about 15 minutes

Calories per serving *323*
Total fat *8 g (23%)*
Saturated fat *2 g*
Protein *29 g*
Carbohydrate *36 g*
Cholesterol *79 mg*
Vitamins *A, B group, C, E*
Minerals *Calcium,
Potassium, Iron, Zinc,
Selenium, Iodine*

2 tablespoons peanut oil
2 shallots, thinly sliced
1 garlic clove, finely chopped
2 large red chilies, seeded and finely chopped
3 cups cold plain boiled rice
1 tablespoon tomato paste
1 tablespoon light soy sauce
salt and pepper
1 tablespoon finely chopped ginger

2 tablespoons chopped scallions
2 tablespoons chopped cilantro leaves
2 tablespoons nam pla fish sauce
12 raw jumbo shrimp, shelled and deveined
8 ounces cod fillets, cut into pieces about ½ inch square
2 large red tomatoes, peeled and quartered
9 small scallops
few sprigs of cilantro leaves to garnish

1 To make the fried rice: heat 1 tablespoon of the oil in a wok and stir-fry the shallots, garlic, and chilies for 2 minutes. Add the cold rice. Turn, toss, and stir the mixture for 2 minutes. Add the tomato paste and soy sauce. Stir to mix well with the rice. Add salt and pepper, taste, and adjust the seasoning. Remove from the heat while you cook the seafood.

2 In another wok or frying pan, heat the remaining oil and stir-fry the ginger, scallions, and cilantro leaves for a minute or so. Add the fish sauce, shrimp, and cod. Cook for 2 minutes, stirring occasionally. Add the tomatoes and scallops, and stir-fry for 2 more minutes. Adjust the seasoning.

3 Give the mixture one good stir, then transfer it to the wok that contains the fried rice. Heat gently, stirring carefully, for 1 to 2 minutes. Alternatively, heat the fried rice in the other wok and, when hot, transfer it to a large platter or a bowl. Arrange the seafood on top of the rice, garnish with cilantro leaves, and serve immediately.

KHAO MAN
Coconut Rice

SERVES 4-6

PREPARATION
about 5 minutes
COOKING
about 20 minutes

In Thailand and elsewhere in Asia, coconut rice is boiled in thick coconut milk. Here, however, to reduce saturated fat and calories, the rice is boiled in water or stock with a little coconut milk. This dish is very popular in the West, partly because to enhance the taste of the coconut milk we add something that Southeast Asians never use when cooking rice in plain water – namely, salt.

1 tablespoon vegetable oil
2 cups jasmine rice, washed and drained
2 cups water or chicken or vegetable stock

¼ cup of coconut milk
1 teaspoon salt
strips of red and green chili, to garnish (optional)

1   Heat the oil in a saucepan and add the rice. Stir until all the grains are coated with the oil. Add the water or stock, coconut milk, and salt. Bring to a boil, and stir the rice once with a wooden spoon. Simmer until all the liquid is absorbed by the rice.

2   Give the rice another stir. Turn down the heat as low as possible. Cover the pan tightly and leave the rice undisturbed for 8 to 10 minutes. Then, still with the cover on tight, take the saucepan from the heat, put it on top of a wet cloth, and leave it undisturbed for 5 minutes.

3   Transfer the rice to a bowl and garnish with strips of chili if you like. Serve hot.

Calories per serving *206*
Total fat *2 g (10%)*
Saturated fat *0.5 g*
Protein *4 g*
Carbohydrate *42 g*
Cholesterol *None*
Vitamins *B3*
Minerals *Potassium, Iron*

EGG NOODLES WITH TOFU

Dried egg noodles are perfectly satisfactory for a dish such as this. Use the firm, fresh Chinese tofu (bean curd), and for best results cook the noodles and tofu separately. Bring them together just before you serve the dish, hot, for lunch or supper.

8 ounces dried egg noodles
½ teaspoon salt
3 tablespoons peanut oil
4 shallots, thinly sliced
2 garlic cloves, thinly sliced
½-inch piece of fresh ginger, finely chopped
2 tablespoons light soy sauce

2 fresh tomatoes, peeled and chopped
2 red chilies, seeded and finely chopped
2 tablespoons yellow bean sauce
7-ounce block of Chinese-style tofu, cut into
16 cubes
2 eggs, lightly beaten
3 tablespoons chopped scallions

SERVES 4

PREPARATION
about 20 minutes
COOKING
about 15 minutes

Calories per serving *567*
Total fat *25 g (39%)*
Saturated fat *4 g*
Protein *35 g*
Carbohydrate *58 g*
Cholesterol *133 mg*
Vitamins *A, B group, C, E*
Minerals *Calcium, Potassium, Iron, Zinc, Iodine*

1   Cook the noodles: boil 5 cups water with the salt and add the noodles. While they are boiling, separate them with a large fork so that they cook evenly and don't stick together. Let them boil for 3 minutes, then transfer them to a colander and put them under cold running water until they are cool. Leave them in the colander to drain completely.

2   Heat half the oil in a wok and stir-fry the shallots, garlic, and ginger for 2 minutes. Add the soy sauce and tomatoes, and stir for 30 seconds.

3   Add the cold noodles and keep turning and tossing them around until they are hot again.

Remove the wok from the heat and cover it, so that the noodles stay warm.

4   In another wok or frying pan, heat the remaining oil and add the chopped chilies and yellow bean sauce. Stir for 2 minutes. Then add the tofu and keep stirring for 2 more minutes. Raise the heat and add the lightly beaten eggs and scallions. With a wooden spoon, vigorously stir the mixture until the eggs are scrambled.

5   Transfer the tofu mixture to the wok with the noodles. Heat together over a low heat, stirring and mixing so that everything is evenly hot. Serve at once.

Overleaf left to right: Fried Rice with Seafood, Egg Noodles with Tofu, Coconut Rice

RICE NOODLES WITH FISH CURRY

SERVES 4-6

PREPARATION
*about 5 minutes, plus
preparing the curry*
COOKING
*about 15 minutes,
plus cooking the curry*

Calories per serving *391*
Total fat *3 g (6%)*
Saturated fat *0.5 g*
Protein *28 g*
Carbohydrate *64 g*
Cholesterol *17 mg*
Vitamins *A, B₁, B₃,
Folic Acid, C, E*
Minerals *Potassium, Iron,
Zinc, Iodine*

1 pound rice vermicelli
5 cups hot water
1 quantity Fish Curry (page 124)

For the garnish:
4 ounces bean sprouts, blanched for 1 minute
2 tablespoons crisp-fried shallots (see page 149)
2 tablespoons chopped cilantro leaves

1 Put the vermicelli into a large bowl or saucepan and pour the hot water over them to cover. Cover and leave them undisturbed for 15 minutes. Drain, and arrange in clusters on a large serving plate.

2 Put the curry and garnishes in separate bowls and invite your guests to help themselves.

FRIED EGG NOODLES WITH CRAB AND SHRIMP

The most satisfactory noodles to use here are Chinese egg noodles, readily available in Asian supermarkets. From experience, I have found that other egg noodles tend to be heavy when cooked. I am told that the Chinese, who have been producing egg noodles of this type for centuries, have the secret of making them with just the right elasticity, neither brittle nor heavy—as long as they are not overcooked.

SERVES 4
as a one-dish meal

PREPARATION
about 25 minutes
COOKING
15-20 minutes

Calories per serving *343*
Total fat *12 g (32%)*
Saturated fat *3 g*
Protein *15 g*
Carbohydrate *46 g*
Cholesterol *42 mg*
Vitamins *B₁, B₂, B₃, B₆,
Folic Acid*
Minerals *Potassium, Iron,
Zinc*

8 ounces dried egg noodles
1 teaspoon salt
2 tablespoons peanut or vegetable oil
4 shallots or 1 medium-sized onion, finely chopped
2 garlic cloves, finely chopped
1-inch piece of fresh ginger, finely chopped
1 tablespoon nam pla fish sauce
1 tablespoon light soy sauce

1 tablespoon fermented yellow bean paste
½ teaspoon freshly ground white pepper
1 teaspoon sugar (optional)
4 tablespoons hot water or chicken stock
4-6 ounces crabmeat (white meat only)
6 ounces small peeled cooked shrimp
2 tablespoons chopped scallions
2 tablespoons chopped cilantro leaves

1 First cook the noodles: heat 5 cups water with the salt and, as soon as it boils, add the noodles. Stir for 3 minutes. Drain in a colander, and run cold water over them, at the same time pulling them apart so that they do not stick to each other too much. The cold water will stop the noodles from cooking and swelling further. Set the noodles aside.

2 A large wok is the best utensil for the stir-frying. Heat the oil in it and stir-fry the shallots or onion and the garlic and ginger for 2 to 3 minutes. Add the fish sauce, soy sauce, yellow bean paste, pepper, sugar (if using it), and the water or stock. Stir until hot, then add the noodles. Keep stirring and scooping the noodles to mix them in well.

3 Add the crabmeat and shrimp, and continue stirring and mixing for 2 minutes longer. Add the scallions and cilantro leaves. Stir again and adjust the seasoning. Serve immediately.

Rice Noodles with Fish Curry

CELLOPHANE NOODLES WITH SHRIMP AND SCALLOPS

This refreshing, clean-tasting salad is delicious as a first course and satisfying as a one-dish lunch. You can replace the scallops with a whole skinless chicken breast fillet, poached for 12 minutes in salted water and then cut into strips when cool. Omit the mooli and serve on a bed of watercress.

SERVES 6-8
as a starter, or 4-6 as a one-dish lunch

PREPARATION
about 30 minutes, plus 15 minutes' soaking
COOKING
about 3 minutes

Calories per serving *247*
Total fat *1 g (5%)*
Saturated fat *0.3 g*
Protein *21 g*
Carbohydrate *37 g*
Cholesterol *35 mg*
Vitamins *A, B group, C*
Minerals *Potassium, Iron, Zinc, Selenium, Iodine*

¼ ounce dried wood ear mushrooms
7 ounces cellophane noodles
3 ounces peeled mooli (white radish)
salt
16 small scallops, with or without the corals
1½ ounces shallots, sliced
½ large red onion, thinly sliced
1½ ounces scallions, thinly sliced
handful of celery leaves (tender inner leaves)

4 tablespoons nam pla fish sauce
4 tablespoons lime juice
1 tablespoon sugar
4-6 small red bird chilies, finely chopped
16 cooked peeled shrimp
4 ounces chopped cilantro leaves, plus more for garnish
more red and green chilies, seeded and sliced, for garnish

1 Soak the wood ears in warm water for about 15 minutes. Rinse and slice them into thin strips, then set aside.

2 Pour boiling water over the noodles and let them stand for 5 minutes. Drain and, using scissors, cut them into short lengths (say 3 to 4 inches).

3 Slice the mooli very thinly, then cut these slices into very narrow strips. Put the strips in a bowl of iced water and set aside.

4 Half fill a saucepan with water and bring to a boil. Add 1 teaspoon of salt and the scallops. Simmer for 2 minutes. Then, with a slotted spoon, transfer the scallops to a plate and leave to cool.

5 Mix the shallots, onions, scallions, celery leaves, and wood ears. Add the fish sauce, lime juice, sugar and chopped chilies. Everything up to this point can be done well ahead of time and kept in the refrigerator.

6 About 10 minutes before serving, drain the shredded mooli and mix it with the noodles. In a large bowl, toss the noodles with the other ingredients, including the shrimp and cilantro leaves, so that they are well mixed. Arrange the salad on a large platter and garnish with more cilantro leaves and chili slices. Serve at room temperature.

Cellophane Noodles with Shrimp and Scallops

Curries

The piquancy of Thai curries is quite different from that of curries made in Malaysia or Indonesia. Many of the ingredients, such as coriander and cumin seeds, are roasted or dry-fried, which brings Thailand closer to Sri Lanka in this respect. Hotness comes mainly from chili, as one would expect, and is therefore easily adjusted to suit your taste or that of your guests; there is little or no ginger. The Thai love of sourness is expressed in the use of galingale, lemongrass, and kaffir lime leaves.

The secret of good curry is the paste—the particular mix of herbs, spices, and seasonings that is needed for the curry you are making. In a traditional kitchen, the fresh spices would be ground in a mortar, or under a stone roller, until they were powder; the process might take most of the morning. Even in the Asia of forty years ago people could see advantages in buying their curry pastes and powders ready-made from the local market, and today these are big business. However, making your own curry paste guarantees flavor and freshness. Spices have a long shelf life, as they don't actually go bad in storage, but they do lose taste and aroma, which are precisely the qualities for which you buy spices. In any case, no store-bought mixture that I know of has the right combination of ingredients for the specifically Thai curries that I am going to describe. With strong red meat, commercial pastes and powders may be adequate, but for fish, shellfish, and vegetables we need something more subtle. My recipes will give you a good start, but in the long run your own judgment, based on what your taste buds prefer, is the only acceptable guide.

The traditional Thai curry is usually cooked with coconut milk, and the sauce can be anything from quite thick to rather runny—even as thin as soup. For a sauce lower in calories and saturated fat, replace the coconut milk with water or stock, and toward the end of cooking add 4 to 5 tablespoons of plain low-fat yogurt. Note, however, that there are a few ingredients, such as pineapple, that do not go well with yogurt. In these cases, just use water and reduce the sauce by cooking it longer, or add 2 tablespoons of chopped creamed coconut at the end of cooking.

Red Curry of Vegetables (page 118)

GREEN CURRY PASTE

This amount is adequate for a chicken curry for 10 to 12 people as a main course, to be eaten with rice and a vegetable dish or a green salad. For curry for 4 people, use 4 tablespoonfuls of paste. Freeze the unused paste by putting 1 tablespoonful into each compartment of an ice-cube tray. Freeze for at least 24 hours, then take the cubes from the tray and store them in a freezer bag. Use within 3 months.

By freezing what you don't use in an ice-cube tray, you are ready to make your next curry with very little preparation, and you can soon build up a treasury of curry flavors in your freezer. When you want to cook, you can drop a cube straight into your saucepan or frying pan—it doesn't need to be thawed first. You can also drop a curry cube into any stir-fried vegetable dish and quickly get all the flavors and the goodness of shallots, garlic, and spices without any extra work.

MAKES ABOUT 2 CUPS

PREPARATION
about 15 minutes
COOKING
35-55 minutes

Calories per tablespoon
15
Total fat *1 g (56%)*
Saturated fat *0.2 g*
Protein *0.5 g*
Carbohydrate *2 g*
Cholesterol *None*
Minerals *Potassium*

3 tablespoons coriander seeds
2 teaspoons cumin seeds
2-4 green chilies, chopped
2 green bell peppers, seeded and chopped
6 shallots, chopped
3 garlic cloves, chopped
1 teaspoon shrimp paste
4 tablespoons chopped cilantro leaves

2 teaspoons chopped cilantro roots (optional)
2 teaspoons chopped lemongrass
½-inch piece of fresh galingale, finely chopped, or 1 teaspoon galingale powder
4 tablespoons tamarind water or 4 tamarind cubes (page 24)
2 tablespoons peanut or vegetable oil
1 teaspoon salt

1 First roast the coriander and cumin seeds in a dry frying pan over moderate heat, stirring frequently, until they just start to brown. Be careful not to burn them or they will taste quite bitter.

2 Put these spices together with all the other ingredients in a blender or food processor with 2 to 3 spoonfuls of water and process for about 2 minutes until you have a smooth, free-flowing paste.

3 Transfer the paste to a saucepan, heat it, and simmer for 5 to 8 minutes, stirring occasionally. Add 1¼ cups of cold water and bring it back to a boil. Cover the pan, then simmer for 30 to 45 minutes.

4 The paste is now ready to use; or it can be stored in a jar in the refrigerator, or frozen as above.

RED CURRY PASTE

MAKES ABOUT 2 CUPS

PREPARATION
about 15 minutes
COOKING
35-50 minutes

Calories etc. as above

3 tablespoons coriander seeds
2 teaspoons cumin seeds
5-10 large red chilies, seeded and chopped
5 shallots, chopped
3 garlic cloves, chopped
1 tablespoon chopped lemongrass

½-inch piece of fresh galingale, finely chopped
3 kaffir lime leaves, chopped
2 teaspoons paprika
2 tablespoons tamarind water
3 tablespoons vegetable oil
1 teaspoon salt

1 First roast the coriander and cumin seeds as described opposite.

2 Put them with all the other ingredients plus 4 tablespoons of water in a blender or food processor and blend for 2 minutes or so until smooth.

3 Transfer to a saucepan and cook, stirring frequently, for 4 minutes. Add 1¼ cups of water, bring the paste to a boil, and cover the pan. Simmer for 30 to 45 minutes. The paste is now ready to be used as directed in the recipes.

4 If the paste is not all to be used at once, leave it to cool and then store it in a jar in the refrigerator or freeze in ice-cube trays as described in the recipe for Green Curry paste opposite.

MASAMAN CURRY PASTE

"Masaman" is the Thai pronunciation of Muslim, and this paste is generally used with beef. Like other curry pastes, it can conveniently be kept as ice cubes in the freezer. One cube is equivalent to one tablespoon of curry paste. Put one or two cubes in a wok, thaw them over moderate heat, and use the paste as a base for any vegetable stir-fry. With a little water added, it makes a liquid for braising fish steaks or tofu.

3 tablespoons coriander seeds
2 teaspoons cumin seeds
2 cloves
½ teaspoon cardamom seeds
6-12 dried large red chilies, soaked in hot water for 5 minutes
½-inch piece of fresh galingale, chopped

2 teaspoons chopped lemongrass
1 teaspoon chopped kaffir lime peel
3 cilantro roots, finely chopped
1 teaspoon salt
2 teaspoons palm or brown sugar
2 tablespoons vegetable oil
3 tablespoons tamarind water

MAKES ABOUT 2 CUPS

PREPARATION
about 20 minutes
COOKING
35-50 minutes

Calories per tablespoon
11
Total fat *1 g (78%)*
Saturated fat *0.2 g*
Protein *0.2 g*
Carbohydrate *1 g*
Cholesterol *None*
Minerals *Potassium*

1 First roast the coriander and cumin seeds as described opposite.

2 Put them with all the other ingredients plus 3 tablespoons of water in a blender or food processor and blend until smooth.

3 Transfer the paste to a saucepan and cook, stirring frequently, for 4 minutes. Add 1¼ cups of water, cover the pan, and continue to cook the paste for 30 to 45 minutes. The paste is now ready to be used as directed in the recipes.

4 If the paste is not all to be used at once, leave it to cool and then store it in a jar in the refrigerator or freeze it in ice-cube trays as described at the top of the opposite page.

CURRY OF GREEN JACKFRUIT

SERVES 4
*as a vegetable dish
with a rice meal*

PREPARATION
about 15 minutes
COOKING
35-55 minutes

Calories per serving *220*
Total fat *11 g (45%)*
Saturated fat *11 g*
Protein *4 g*
Carbohydrate *28 g*
Cholesterol *None*
Vitamins *Folate, C*
Minerals *Potassium, Iron,
Zinc*

In most Western cities, a good Thai or Indian food shop will take your order for fresh green jackfruit. It will come in thick slices, already peeled. Be careful of the sticky juice: it will leave a permanent dark stain if it gets on your clothes. The stickiness on your hands can be washed away by rubbing with cooking oil and then washing with plenty of soapy water. Alternatively, use canned green jackfruit, which is easily available in Asian markets.

1 pound fresh or drained canned green jackfruit
6-8 tablespoons Masaman Curry Paste (page 117)
1¼ cups hot water
2 tablespoons chopped creamed coconut

salt and pepper
handful of mint leaves, to garnish
2 tablespoons roasted peanuts, roughly crushed, to garnish (optional)

1 If you are using fresh fruit, cut each round slice into 4 pieces. Boil in slightly salted water for 8 to 10 minutes. Canned fruit need only be rinsed.

2 Put the curry paste in a saucepan, and cook for 3 minutes, stirring frequently. Add the hot water. Bring to a boil and simmer for 20 minutes.

3 Add the jackfruit and cook for 10 to 15 minutes, stirring from time to time. Stir in the coconut.

4 Adjust the seasoning and sprinkle the garnish on top. Serve hot with rice.

RED CURRY OF VEGETABLES

SERVES 4-6

PREPARATION
about 15 minutes
COOKING
about 25 minutes

Calories per serving *119*
Total fat *6 g (46%)*
Saturated fat *3 g*
Protein *5 g*
Carbohydrate *15 g*
Cholesterol *None*
Vitamins *B1, B6, Folate, E*
Minerals *Calcium,
Potassium, Zinc*

Don't think that a delicious curry is merely the result of combining different spices. Curry paste won't taste good without salt, sugar, and tamarind water or lime juice. Also, a long-cooked meat curry will be tastier than a short-cooked one, because the meat juices will enhance the sauce and the meat will absorb the spices. In the same way, curried vegetables will be tastier than cooked vegetables with a curry dressing. (See page 115)

4 tablespoons Red Curry Paste (page 116)
2½ cups hot water
salt and pepper
*½ pound yard-long beans or green beans, cut into
1-inch lengths*

8 ounces peeled waxy potatoes, cut into sticks
8 ounces cauliflower florets
8 ounces parsnips, cut into sticks
2 tablespoons chopped creamed coconut
handful each of basil and cilantro leaves

1 Put the curry paste in a saucepan, stir-fry it for 2 minutes, then add the hot water and some salt and pepper. Simmer for 6 minutes.

2 Bring the sauce to boiling point, add the beans and potatoes, and cook for 6 to 8 minutes. Then add the cauliflower and parsnips. Cover the pan, leaving the lid slightly ajar. Simmer the vegetable stew for 5 to 6 minutes more. Adjust the seasoning.

3 Add the chopped creamed coconut and the basil and cilantro leaves and stir once. Simmer for 1 more minute. Serve immediately, as a vegetable accompaniment to a rice or noodle dish.

RED CURRY OF STUFFED SQUID

Small squid are natural containers for stuffings. In Thailand stuffed squid are usually served cold, sliced very thin. The stuffing looks very much like sausage meat, and traditionally contains pork and pork fat. In this book we are avoiding pork and other fatty meats, so here I use the other traditional Asian filling, shrimp paste. This consists of fresh shrimp, chopped or blended with some other simple ingredients.

8 baby squid, cleaned and the tentacles finely chopped

For the stuffing:
12 ounces raw shrimp without heads, shelled and deveined
1 egg white
1 teaspoon salt
½ teaspoon sugar
2 teaspoons potato flour
2 garlic cloves, finely chopped
1-inch piece of fresh ginger, finely chopped

For the curry sauce:
8 tablespoons Red Curry Paste (page 116)
1 cup hot water
2-3 tablespoons plain low-fat yogurt

For the garnish:
peel of 1 lime, cut into tiny strips and immersed in
1 tablespoonful of nam pla fish sauce
3 teaspoons finely chopped lemongrass
3 tablespoons peanut oil
handful of chopped cilantro leaves

1 Put all the ingredients for the stuffing in a blender or food processor and blend to a smooth paste. Transfer the mixture to a bowl, add the chopped squid tentacles, and mix well.

2 Prepare the lime peel for the garnish: drain the strips of lime peel, discard the fish sauce, and dry the peel with paper towels. Heat the oil in a small saucepan and fry the lime peel, stirring all the time, for about 1 minute. Drain on paper towels. Discard the oil.

3 Fill the squid with the stuffing—not too full, as the stuffing expands when it is cooked. Secure the top with toothpicks.

4 Make the curry sauce: put the curry paste in a saucepan, and heat and stir for 2 minutes or a little longer. Add the hot water and bring to just below a boil. Add the yogurt a spoonful at a time, stirring continuously until you have mixed it all in. Lower the heat a little, add the stuffed squid, and simmer for 4 to 6 minutes. Adjust the seasoning.

5 Transfer the squid to a flat plate, remove the toothpicks, and cut each squid in half lengthwise. Arrange the squid halves on a deep plate and pour the curry sauce over them. Sprinkle the garnishes on top, and serve hot with rice and vegetables.

SERVES 4

PREPARATION
about 35 minutes
COOKING
about 15 minutes

Calories per serving *301*
Total fat *16 g (35%)*
Saturated fat *3 g*
Protein *56 g*
Carbohydrate *10 g*
Cholesterol *729 mg*
Vitamins *B group*
Minerals *Calcium, Potassium, Iron, Zinc, Selenium, Iodine*

Overleaf: Curry of Green Jackfruit, Red Curry of Stuffed Squid

GAENG PED SAPPAROT
Duck Curry with Pineapple

In Thailand, where duck curry is a popular everyday home-cooked dish, it is usually made with fresh whole duck or with Chinese roast duck—the kind you see hanging from hooks in the windows of Chinese restaurants and food stores. The duck will be cut into 10 or 12 pieces, bones and all, and then cooked in the curry sauce. The pineapple is added to the curry just before serving. However, as this is usually intended for a big family dinner, here I suggest you make it simply with duck breasts. The pineapple must, of course, still be fresh, not canned. Use the remains of the pineapple as fruit for dessert.

8 tablespoons Red Curry Paste (page 116)
2 whole duck breasts, each half skinned and cut across at an angle into 4 slices
¾ cup hot water
2 tablespoons tomato paste
salt and pepper
3 tablespoons chopped creamed coconut
¼ large pineapple or 1 miniature pineapple, peeled and cut into bite-sized pieces
large handful of basil leaves

SERVES 4

PREPARATION
about 10 minutes, plus 2 hours' marinating
COOKING
about 20 minutes

Calories per serving *197*
Total fat *9 g (42%)*
Saturated fat *2 g*
Protein *21 g*
Carbohydrate *9 g*
Cholesterol *110 mg*
Vitamins *B group*
Minerals *Potassium, Iron, Zinc*

1 Put 2 tablespoonfuls of the curry paste in a bowl, add the duck slices, mix them well, and leave to marinate for at least 2 hours, or overnight in the refrigerator.
2 When ready to cook, take the duck out of the refrigerator. Put the remaining curry paste in a saucepan. Cook, stirring all the time, for 2 minutes, then add the marinated slices of duck. Continue stirring for 2 more minutes. Add the hot water and tomato paste, and stir well to mix them. Bring to a boil, cover the pan, and let simmer for 4 minutes. Then lower the heat and simmer, uncovered, for 8 minutes, stirring from time to time. Adjust the seasoning.
3 About 2 minutes before you plan to serve the curry, add the creamed coconut and stir to dissolve it. Then add the pineapple pieces and basil leaves. Serve piping hot, with plain boiled rice accompanied by some cooked vegetables or a salad with more fresh uncooked pineapple in it.

Duck Curry with Pineapple

GREEN CURRY WITH CHICKEN

This, the best known of all Thai curries, is sometimes called green chicken curry. I don't call it that myself because I really don't like the idea of a "green chicken."

SERVES 4

PREPARATION
about 15 minutes
COOKING
about 40 minutes

Calories per serving *152*
Total fat *3 g (18%)*
Saturated fat *1 g*
Protein *19 g*
Carbohydrate *14 g*
Cholesterol *47 mg*
Vitamins *B group, C*
Minerals *Potassium, Iron, Iodine*

1 whole chicken breast and 4 thighs, all skin removed
8 ounces pea eggplants or small new potatoes

For the garnish:
3 small green chilies, seeded and chopped
handful of cilantro leaves

For the sauce:
8 tablespoons Green Curry Paste (page 116)
3¾ cups hot water
4 tablespoons plain low-fat yogurt
juice of ½ lime
salt and pepper

1 Cut the chicken meat into ½-inch cubes. If using pea eggplants, pick them from the stalks and discard the stalks. Set aside.
2 Put the curry paste in a saucepan and heat, stirring, for 2 minutes. Add the chicken pieces, and stir them around over low heat until all are coated by the paste. Add the hot water, bring to a boil, and simmer, uncovered, for 20 minutes.

3 Add the yogurt a spoonful at a time, stirring continuously until it is all incorporated into the sauce. Bring the curry back to a boil, add the eggplants or new potatoes, and continue to cook over medium heat for 15 minutes. Add the lime juice; taste and add some salt and pepper if needed.
4 Serve hot, garnished with green chilies and cilantro leaves.

FISH CURRY

I can think of only a few vegetables that are really satisfactory for a fish curry and one of them is spinach. So here is a white fish and green spinach curry.

SERVES 4

PREPARATION
about 10 minutes
COOKING
about 20 minutes

Calories per serving *178*
Total fat *3 g (17%)*
Saturated fat *1 g*
Protein *32 g*
Carbohydrate *6 g*
Cholesterol *25 mg*
Vitamins *A, B group, C, E*
Minerals *Calcium, Potassium, Iron, Zinc, Iodine*

6-8 tablespoons Green Curry Paste (page 116)
2½ cups hot water
salt and pepper
4 tablespoons plain low-fat yogurt

4 monkfish tails or cod or ocean perch fillets, each weighing about 6 ounces
juice of ½ lime or 1 tablespoon tamarind water
1 pound young spinach leaves

1 Heat the curry paste in a saucepan and let it simmer, stirring all the time, for 2 minutes. Add the hot water and some salt and pepper, and continue to simmer for 8 minutes, stirring frequently. Add the yogurt a spoonful at a time, continuing to stir until you have mixed it all in.
2 Bring the sauce almost to the boiling point and

add the fish fillets. Cook for 4 minutes, then turn the fish over. Add the lime juice or tamarind water and the spinach. Continue to cook, uncovered, for 4 more minutes. With a wooden spoon, carefully push the spinach down into the sauce. Adjust the seasoning and serve hot with rice or noodles.

EGGPLANT AND EGG CURRY

Unfortunately, the large, bulbous purple eggplant is not really suitable here. In Thailand there are several small eggplant varieties, one of which is actually white and about the size and shape of a large hen's egg. Sometimes this white eggplant is available in American stores, but the kind that is almost always obtainable is the long, slim Chinese or Japanese eggplant, which will do very well for this curry. The taste is slightly bitter, and the texture gives a wonderful contrast to the eggs.

8 tablespoons Green or Red Curry Paste (page 116)
3-5 small green or red bird chilies, chopped
1 tablespoon tamarind water
2½ cups hot water
12 small new potatoes, well scrubbed
3 tablespoons plain low-fat yogurt

8 hard-boiled eggs, shelled
8 white or greenish white small eggplants, halved, or 4 Chinese or Japanese eggplants, chopped
salt and pepper
handful of mint
handful of cilantro leaves

SERVES 4

PREPARATION
about 15 minutes
COOKING
about 30 minutes, plus cooking the eggs

1 Heat the curry paste in a saucepan and let it simmer, stirring all the time, for 2 minutes. Add the chopped chilies and the tamarind water. Continue to simmer for 2 more minutes, then add the hot water. Bring the mixture back to a boil, then add the potatoes and cook for 8 to 10 minutes.

2 Add the yogurt a spoonful at a time, stirring continuously until you have mixed it all in. Simmer for 5 more minutes. Add the eggs and eggplant and continue to cook over medium heat for 10 more minutes. Adjust the seasoning.

3 Add the mint and cilantro leaves, and simmer for 1 minute more. Serve piping hot, with rice and cooked vegetables or salad.

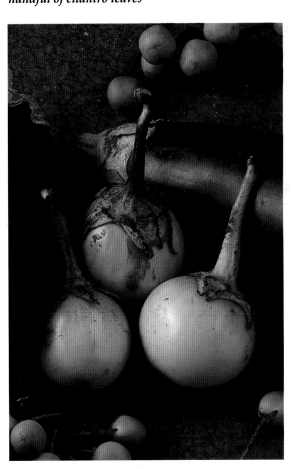

Calories per serving *320*
Total fat *14 g (40%)*
Saturated fat *4 g*
Protein *18 g*
Carbohydrate *33 g*
Cholesterol *386 mg*
Vitamins *A, B group, C, E*
Minerals *Calcium, Potassium, Iron, Zinc, Selenium, Iodine*

Vegetarian Dishes

I hope I would never serve any food to a vegetarian that I would not also serve to a non-vegetarian at the same table; all the dishes in this section are delicious in their own right. I do not know what percentage of the Thai population is vegetarian, but I would guess it is not very large. In Southeast Asia generally vegetarianism is well understood, but not widely practiced. Families, until recently, were usually large and the food supply was uncertain; even now, one cannot be too confident of the future. In such circumstances, most people will not willingly avoid any nutritious food, as long as it is not forbidden outright by their religion.

If you are a vegetarian by conviction, in the sense of not wishing to eat any creature that has been killed, you will probably find that you don't want to eat regular Thai food at all. It is quite difficult to find a vegetable dish that does not include a small amount of finely chopped meat or shrimp or fish. Almost all use nam pla fish sauce, shrimp paste, or dried shrimps. The Buddhist religion discourages killing, but does not forbid the eating of meat and fish.

For those who are strict vegetarians, however, the amazing soybean was perceived long ago as exceptionally good food value, and science has confirmed that its proteins make up for those that are lacking in rice. One way of making them available to us is by extracting and curdling soy milk, which then becomes bean curd, or tofu. Consequently, tofu plays a large part in this section.

No recipe in this section uses fish sauce, shrimp paste, or dried shrimps. Their place is taken by soy sauce and fermented bean paste or bean sauce. Most of these recipes are suitable for vegans, or could be easily adapted. I am not acquainted with any Thai vegans, but life as a vegan in the tropics is probably simpler than anywhere else, if only because there are plenty of coconuts.

Stir-fried Mixed Vegetables (page 128)

STIR-FRIED MIXED VEGETABLES

I first heard of the "Royal Project" for growing fruit and vegetables in Chiang Mai during a visit to Thailand in 1991. Norbert Kostner, the executive chef of the Oriental Hotel in Bangkok, has been closely involved since 1969 in setting up and fostering the production of these beautiful miniature vegetables and salad leaves: arugula, lollo rosso, and different varieties of spinach, as well as the finest Italian San Marzano tomatoes. Now, in winter, we can get baby corn and elegant slim asparagus, flown in from Thailand and displayed in our supermarkets. So you have plenty of choice for this dish. (See previous page.)

SERVES 4-6

PREPARATION
about 20 minutes
COOKING
about 15 minutes

Calories per serving *92*
Total fat *6 g (60%)*
Saturated fat *1 g*
Protein *3 g*
Carbohydrate *6 g*
Cholesterol *None*
Vitamins *A, B1, B2, B6,*
Folate, C, E
Minerals *Potassium, Iron,*
Zinc

6 ounces slim asparagus stalks
6 ounces baby corn
4 ounces snow peas
1 large yellow bell pepper
6 ounces very small button mushrooms
3 tablespoons peanut oil
3 shallots, thinly sliced

1 red chili, seeded and chopped
½-inch piece of fresh ginger, thinly sliced
1 teaspoon palm sugar or brown granulated sugar
4 tablespoons hot water
2 tablespoons chopped cilantro leaves, plus more
whole leaves for garnish
salt and pepper

1 Prepare the vegetables: cut off the tips of the asparagus and reserve. Slice each stalk in half at an angle. Cut the corn in halves lengthwise. The snow peas can be left whole, or if they are rather large, cut them in half on the slant. Halve and seed the bell pepper, then cut it into about 8 or 10 slices. Wipe the mushrooms.

2 In a wok or a large shallow saucepan, heat the oil and stir-fry the shallots, chili, and ginger for a minute or two. Add the sugar, stir once or twice, then add the sliced asparagus stalks, button mushrooms, and corn. Stir again and add the hot water. Lower the heat, cover the pan, and simmer for 3 minutes.

3 Uncover the pan and add the chopped cilantro leaves, snow peas, bell pepper, asparagus tips, and salt and pepper. Continue to stir-fry for 2 minutes. Adjust the seasoning and stir-fry the vegetables for about 3 minutes more. Serve hot, garnished with some whole cilantro leaves.

STEAMED STUFFED TOFU

This dish is definitely Chinese in origin, and in China the stuffed tofu is usually steamed first, then deep-fried and served with soy sauce or chili bean paste. There are many variations, however, and this healthy Thai version, which involves no deep-frying, is served as a warm salad with a characteristic Thai dressing.

2 squares of fresh Chinese-style tofu
4 scallions, cut into fine julienne strips
2 tablespoons fine julienne strips of fresh ginger
2 tablespoons peanut oil
1 teaspoon sesame oil
2 tablespoons finely chopped roasted or fried peanuts (optional)

For the stuffing:
about ½ cup unsalted dry-roasted cashew nuts, coarsely chopped
2 tablespoons finely chopped scallions
1 tablespoon finely chopped cilantro leaves

salt and pepper
white of 1 egg

For the salad:
4 plump tomatoes, peeled and quartered
handful of watercress, trimmed
½ cucumber, peeled and thinly sliced

For the dressing:
2 tablespoons light soy sauce
2 tablespoons lime juice
1 tablespoon superfine sugar
2 small red bird chilies, finely chopped or crushed

SERVES 4
as a starter or light lunch

PREPARATION
about 30 minutes
COOKING
about 7 minutes

Calories per serving *349*
Total fat *18 g (47%)*
Saturated fat *2 g*
Protein *29 g*
Carbohydrate *21 g*
Cholesterol *None*
Vitamins *A, C, E, B6, B12*
Minerals *Calcium, Iron, Potassium*

1 Cut each square of the tofu into 4 smaller squares. Set these 8 pieces aside. They will later be sandwiched together, with the stuffing in the middle.

2 Put all the ingredients for the stuffing into a bowl, adding the egg white last. Then mix and whisk the stuffing very briskly with a fork until all the ingredients are well combined.

3 With a teaspoon, put equal quantities of the stuffing on 4 of the tofu slices. Spread the stuffing evenly with a knife, then put the other slice of tofu on top. Keep the 4 tofu sandwiches in the refrigerator in a bowl wrapped in plastic wrap .

4 When you are ready to serve, steam the stuffed tofu for 4 minutes either in a steamer or on a plate set on another upturned plate in the bottom of a covered pan with a little water. Keep warm.

5 Divide the salad mixture among 4 plates. Combine the dressing ingredients and spoon the dressing over each salad. Put a piece of stuffed tofu on each plate, on top of the salad. Put equal amounts of julienned scallion and ginger on each piece of stuffed tofu.

6 Heat the peanut and sesame oils together in a small saucepan. When the oil is hot, pour it evenly over the scallions and ginger. Sprinkle the chopped peanuts, if using, over the top and serve immediately.

Overleaf left to right: Water Spinach with Marinated Steamed Tofu (page 132), Steamed Stuffed Tofu

WATER SPINACH WITH MARINATED STEAMED TOFU

The best tofu to use here is the firm, fresh Chinese kind, or the so-called original tofu that is now sold in large supermarkets and health food stores. Instead of water spinach, you can use large spinach leaves (but not baby spinach). If you cannot get these either, use Swiss chard. (See page 130.)

SERVES 4

PREPARATION
*about 20 minutes,
plus 2 hours'
marinating*
COOKING
about 10 minutes

Calories per serving *202*
Total fat *13 g (56%)*
Saturated fat *2 g*
Protein *16 g*
Carbohydrate *7 g*
Cholesterol *None*
Vitamins *A, B1, B3, B6,
Folic Acid, C, E*
Minerals *Calcium,
Potassium, Iron, Zinc*

1-1½ pounds tofu
2 tablespoons vegetable oil
3 shallots, chopped
2 large green chilies, seeded and thinly sliced
1 pound water spinach or large-leaved ordinary spinach, trimmed
1 tablespoon light soy sauce
¼ teaspoon salt

1 teaspoon sugar

For the marinade:
2 tablespoons chopped scallions
1 tablespoon yellow bean sauce
1 tablespoon light soy sauce
¼ teaspoon chili powder

1 Cut the tofu into quarters and then quarter each quarter again, to make 16 cubes.

2 Put the ingredients for the marinade in a bowl and carefully add the tofu cubes. Turn the tofu over, piece by piece, so that each one is coated with the marinade. Leave to marinate for 2 hours.

3 Arrange the pieces of tofu in a deep plate and steam for 8 minutes either in a steamer or set on an upturned plate in the bottom of a covered pan with a little water.

4 Meanwhile, in a large frying pan or a wok, heat the oil. Fry the shallots and sliced green chilies, stirring often, for 3 minutes. Add the spinach, soy sauce, salt, and sugar. Stir once and cover the pan. Simmer for 3 minutes.

5 Uncover the pan and adjust the seasoning. Transfer the spinach and the cooking juices to a warm platter and arrange the steamed tofu on top. Serve immediately, with rice or noodles.

BROCCOLI AND CASHEW NUTS

In most Southeast Asian countries, broccoli is a newcomer to the tropical vegetable market. It is a good vegetable for mixed stir-frying, Chinese-style, but in Thailand most people prefer their vegetables cooked quite tender, not crunchy. When they want something crunchy they prefer raw vegetables. The cashew nuts used here show an Indian influence.

2 tablespoons Green Curry Paste (page 116)
4 tablespoons plain low-fat yogurt or coconut milk
2 teaspoons light soy sauce

2¼ pounds trimmed broccoli florets
4 ounces unsalted dry-roasted cashew nuts

1 Heat the curry paste in a saucepan and simmer for 2 minutes. Add the yogurt or coconut milk, soy sauce, and broccoli. Cover the pan, lower the heat, and simmer for 15 minutes. Check from time to time to make sure the vegetables are not burning. If necessary, add some hot water.

2 At the end of this time, remove the cover, raise the heat a little, and continue cooking, stirring occasionally, for another 5 minutes.

3 Serve while still hot, strewing the dry-roasted cashew nuts over the broccoli just before serving, so that they stay crunchy and are not softened too much by the effects of the heat and moisture.

SERVES 4-6

PREPARATION
about 5 minutes
COOKING
about 20 minutes

Calories per serving *187*
Total fat *12 g (58%)*
Saturated fat *2 g*
Protein *12 g*
Carbohydrate *8 g*
Cholesterol *None*
Vitamins *A, B1, B6, Folic Acid, C, E*
Minerals *Calcium, Potassium, Iron, Zinc, Iodine*

SWEET-AND-SOUR VEGETABLES WITH PINEAPPLE AND TOFU

Usually the sourness in this dish comes from tamarind water, but the juice of a fresh lime is an excellent substitute. If you are very fond of tamarind, however, then make tamarind water as described on page 25 and store it as ice cubes. For this dish you need 2 tamarind cubes, or 2 tablespoons of tamarind water.

SERVES 4-6

PREPARATION
about 20 minutes
COOKING
about 15 minutes

Calories per serving *94*
Total fat *3 g (31%)*
Saturated fat *0.4 g*
Protein *7 g*
Carbohydrate *10 g*
Cholesterol *None*
Vitamins *B1, B3, B6,*
Folic Acid, C
Minerals *Calcium,*
Potassium, Iron

2 tablespoons light soy sauce
2 tablespoons lime juice or tamarind water
4 tablespoons hot water
1 teaspoon sugar
6 shallots or pearl onions, peeled and halved
4 ounces red cabbage leaves, cut into 1-inch squares
4 ounces white cabbage leaves, cut into 1-inch squares
2 medium yellow or green zucchini, cut into rounds ¼ inch thick

2 large green chilies, seeded and quartered
½ medium-sized pineapple, cut into ½-inch cubes
1 block of Chinese-style tofu, weighing about 12-14 ounces, cut into 16 squares
2 teaspoons chopped lemongrass
½-inch piece of fresh ginger, peeled and chopped
2 tablespoons chopped cilantro leaves, plus a few more whole leaves for garnish (optional)
salt
little chili oil, if necessary

1   Put the soy sauce, lime juice or tamarind water, hot water, and sugar in a large shallow saucepan or wok. Heat almost to boiling point. Add the shallots or pickling onions and simmer for 4 minutes.

2   Add all the vegetables, including the chilies. Cover the pan and simmer for 4 minutes. Stir the mixture once or twice to make sure the pan is not completely dry. Add more hot water if necessary.

3   Uncover the pan and add the pineapple and tofu, with the lemongrass, ginger, and cilantro leaves. Simmer for 3 more minutes, stirring carefully so as not to break up the tofu. Taste and add salt and chili oil if needed.

4   Serve immediately, garnished with a few more cilantro leaves if you like, and accompanied by rice or noodles.

Sweet-and-Sour Vegetables with Pineapple and Tofu

STUFFED EGGPLANT

This is a very typical Thai eggplant dish with a vegetarian stuffing. Round eggplants, which are often white in color, are sometimes available from Asian stores. If you can't find round eggplants, use Japanese or Chinese eggplants; cut them in half lengthwise and stuff them as you would zucchini. The stuffed eggplants are usually deep-fried for 2 to 3 minutes and served, hot or cold, with sweet chili sauce. A healthier cooking method is as follows.

8-12 round eggplants or 4-6 Japanese or Chinese eggplants

For the stuffing:
1 tablespoon vegetable oil
2 shallots, finely chopped
1 large red chili, seeded and chopped
2 small carrots, peeled and diced
2 small parsnips, peeled and diced
1 tablespoon desiccated coconut
1 tablespoon light soy sauce
salt and pepper
1 egg, beaten
sprigs of watercress, spinach, or other green leaves, to garnish

SERVES 4
as a side dish

PREPARATION
about 15 minutes
COOKING
about 30 minutes, plus cooling

Calories per serving *133*
Total fat *7 g (48%)*
Saturated fat *3 g*
Protein *5 g*
Carbohydrate *13 g*
Cholesterol *58 mg*
Vitamins *A, B group, C, E*
Minerals *Potassium, Iron, Iodine*

1 Steam the eggplants whole for 12 minutes. Leave them to get cold.

2 Remove the stems and cut each eggplant in half. With a teaspoon, scoop out the flesh, then chop it finely. Set aside.

3 Make the stuffing: heat the vegetable oil in a frying pan and stir-fry the shallots and chilies for 2 minutes. Add the carrots, parsnips, and coconut. Stir for 1 minute more, then add the soy sauce and 4 tablespoons of water. Simmer, stirring from time to time, for 3 minutes.

4 Add the chopped inner part of the eggplants, and continue cooking for 1 more minute. Adjust the seasoning. Remove the pan from the heat, and leave to cool.

5 When the stuffing is cool, mix in the egg to bind it. Then, with a small spoon, stuff the eggplant halves. Up to this point everything can be prepared well in advance.

6 Arrange the stuffed eggplants on a plate that will go into your steamer or a double saucepan, and steam them for 8 to 10 minutes. Serve them hot or cold, with Sweet Chili Sauce (page 142) spooned on top and garnished with sprigs of greenery.

Stuffed Eggplant

TOFU IN YELLOW BEAN SAUCE

SERVES 4

PREPARATION
about 15 minutes
COOKING
about 10 minutes

Calories per serving *347*
Total fat *23 g (59%)*
Saturated fat *1 g*
Protein *28 g*
Carbohydrate *8 g*
Cholesterol *None*
Vitamins *A, B1, B3, B6,*
Folate
Minerals *Calcium, Iron,*
Zinc

Fermented yellow beans are made from soybeans, as is tofu. The two together in one recipe make a high-protein dish, cooked here without any additional fat. Some Chinese-style tofu is sold ready-fried—use this here.

1 pound fried Chinese-style tofu cubes, each halved into 2 triangles
½ pound yard-long beans or green beans, thinly sliced at an angle
handful of celery leaves
handful of basil leaves

For the sauce:
4 tablespoons fermented yellow bean sauce (page 22)
4 garlic cloves, chopped
1-2 small red bird chilies, chopped
½-inch piece of fresh ginger, finely chopped
2 tablespoons lime juice or tamarind water
½ cup warm water
1 teaspoon sugar

1 Put the sauce ingredients in a blender and blend until smooth. If you prefer a less smooth sauce, just put the ingredients into a bowl and mix well.
2 Transfer the sauce to a saucepan and heat it. When it is hot, add the tofu and the beans. Cover the pan

and simmer for 5 to 6 minutes. By this time the sauce is very thick and reduced.
3 Add most of the celery and basil leaves, shake the pan, and continue to simmer for 1 minute more. Serve hot, garnished with the remaining leaves.

SCRAMBLED TOFU AND EGGS

SERVES 4

PREPARATION
about 15 minutes
COOKING
about 10 minutes,
plus hard-boiling
the eggs

Calories per serving *210*
Total fat *16 g (67%)*
Saturated fat *3 g*
Protein *16 g*
Carbohydrate *2 g*
Cholesterol *212 mg*
Vitamins *A, B group, C, E*
Minerals *Calcium,*
Potassium, Iron, Zinc,
Iodine, Selenium

This is usually eaten for breakfast, with rice, but try it on wheat toast. (You don't need to butter the toast.)

1 block of fresh Chinese-style tofu, weighing about 12-14 ounces
2 tablespoons vegetable oil
1-2 small red bird chilies, chopped
2 shallots, finely chopped
4 ounces button mushrooms, thinly sliced

3 tablespoons chopped scallions
2 tablespoons light soy sauce
4 tablespoons hot water
2 hard-boiled eggs, shelled and quartered
2 eggs, beaten
salt and pepper

1 Wrap the block of tofu in a piece of cheesecloth. Squeeze it to get rid of a little of the excess liquid, while at the same time crumbling the tofu. Transfer the crumbled tofu to a bowl.
2 Heat the oil in a frying pan and fry the chilies, shallots, and mushrooms, stirring them all the time,

for 3 minutes. Add the crumbled tofu, scallions, soy sauce, and hot water. Simmer for 3 minutes, stirring often, then add the hard-boiled eggs.
3 Pour in the beaten eggs and scramble the whole thing with a wooden spoon for 1 to 2 minutes. Taste and season if necessary. Serve immediately.

Tofu in Yellow Bean Sauce

Sauces, Relishes & Pickles

These condiments are an important part of a Thai meal, especially when there are guests. We all have different tastes, and the good cook understands that not everyone wants his food heavily laced with chilies. Even chili lovers welcome a cooling cucumber relish if one of the curries turns out to be hotter than they expected. So a bowl or two of hot relish, and one or two more of sharp-tasting pickles or something soothing, are always at hand.

When you are faced with a big festive spread, remember that you have complete freedom of choice. You are invited to help yourself, and your host or one of the other guests will be very happy to guide you around the table. Along with the principal dishes, you take what you want of the sauces and pickles. If you are eating in a Thai restaurant, you may not be offered any of the relishes or pickles that you will find in this section. If you know what to ask for, however, they will always be brought from the kitchen.

From the cook's point of view, one of the attractions of these sauces is that they can usually be stored for at least a week or two in the refrigerator, and some can be frozen. They can then be used as ingredients in later cooking. In fact, if you have not cooked Thai before, these are a great help in getting started, because you can prepare a sauce well in advance, when you are not too pressed for time, and know that the unfamiliar part of the work—the blending and balancing of exotic ingredients—is safely accomplished.

For example, Fermented Yellow Bean Sauce and Coconut Relish are not only good in themselves as dips but can be used later as sauces in which to cook vegetables. Plain Chili Sauce is best of all to have in your refrigerator, because every time you cook you can use one or two teaspoonfuls of it and not have to spend time seeding two or three fresh chilies.

Clockwise from the top: Plain Chili Sauce, Coconut Relish, Fermented Yellow Bean Sauce (pages 142-3)

PLAIN CHILI SAUCE

MAKES 1¼ CUPS

PREPARATION
about 2 minutes
COOKING
about 10 minutes,
plus cooling

Calories per tablespoon
10

Total fat *0.6 g (61%)*

Saturated fat *0.1 g*

Protein *0.2 g*

Carbohydrate *0.7 g*

Cholesterol *None*

Vitamins *A*

Minerals *Potassium*

I make this plain chili sauce and keep it in the refrigerator to save me seeding and chopping fresh chilies every time I need one or two for a recipe. One teaspoon of this chili sauce is the equivalent of a large chili.

½ pound large red chilies, boiled for 2 minutes
½ teaspoon salt
1 tablespoon vegetable oil
1 tablespoon tamarind water or white vinegar
2 tablespoons hot water
1 whole red chili for garnish (optional)

1 Blend all the ingredients in a blender until smooth. Transfer the mixture to a saucepan and cook on a low heat, stirring frequently, for 8 minutes.
2 Leave the sauce to cool, then store in a jar and refrigerate until needed. You can also freeze this chili sauce in an ice-cube tray, as you can curry paste and tamarind water (see pages 116 and 24).

NAM JEEM
Sweet Chili Sauce

MAKES ABOUT 2½ CUPS

PREPARATION
about 10 minutes
COOKING
about 1 hour, plus
cooling

Calories per tablespoon
10

Total fat *0.6 g (54%)*

Saturated fat *0.1 g*

Protein *0.3 g*

Carbohydrate *1 g*

Cholesterol *None*

Vitamins *A*

Minerals *Potassium*

This is the chili sauce that you get as a dip in almost all Thai restaurants. Presumably it is made in huge quantities in a factory, as it is the only kind that is available in every Thai or Chinese shop and supermarket. It is easy and cheap to make.

1 pound large red chilies, boiled whole for 4 minutes
2 shallots, chopped
2 garlic cloves, chopped

2 tablespoons sugar
1 teaspoon salt
2 tablespoons vegetable oil

1 Put all the ingredients in a food processor with 4 tablespoons water and blend until quite smooth. (The commercial product has the seeds still intact.)
2 Transfer the mixture to a saucepan, bring to a boil, and stir for 2 minutes. Add 2½ cups of water, cover the pan and cook the sauce for 45 to 60 minutes.
3 Leave sauce to cool, and then store it in a large airtight jar in the refrigerator. It will keep in good condition there for 2 weeks or longer.

YELLOW BEAN SAUCE

This is an excellent standby vegetarian sauce, good in the cooking of hard-boiled eggs, tofu, or vegetables. It can also be served hot from the sauceboat to add piquancy to plain boiled rice and steamed vegetables. It will keep fresh in the refrigerator for up to a week. Just heat it before use.

2 tablespoons vegetable oil

3 shallots, finely chopped

2 large red chilies, seeded and finely chopped

½-inch piece of fresh ginger, chopped

1 teaspoon ground coriander seeds

4 tablespoons fermented yellow bean sauce (page 22)

4 tablespoons tamarind water

salt

chopped scallion, to garnish (optional)

1 Heat the oil in a saucepan and stir-fry the shallots and chilies for 2 minutes. Add the ginger and coriander. Continue to stir for a few seconds.

2 Add the bean sauce and stir again, then stir in the tamarind water. Bring the mixture almost to boiling point and simmer for 10 minutes. Taste, and add salt if necessary.

3 Serve immediately, garnished with some sliced spring onion if you like, or store in the refrigerator until needed. Heat the sauce in a pan before serving.

MAKES ½–⅔ CUP

PREPARATION
about 10 minutes
COOKING
about 15 minutes

Calories per tablespoon
50
Total fat *3 g (53%)*
Saturated fat *0.6 g*
Protein *1 g*
Carbohydrate *5 g*
Cholesterol *None*
Vitamins *C*
Minerals *Potassium*

COCONUT RELISH

This coconut relish is not exclusively Thai, as it is popular in Sri Lanka, South India, and most other South Asian countries as well. A good accompaniment to a rice meal, it is also excellent as a dressing for mixed cooked vegetables. It goes without saying that it is better made with freshly grated coconut, though desiccated will do.

1 cup freshly grated or desiccated coconut

1 teaspoon paprika

4 tablespoons hot water

1 teaspoon salt

1 tablespoon chopped chives or scallion

For the paste:

4 shallots, chopped

2 garlic cloves, chopped

½-inch piece of fresh ginger, chopped

2-4 small red chilies, chopped

½-inch piece of fresh galingale, peeled and chopped

2 tablespoons tamarind water

1 tablespoon vegetable oil

1 Put all the ingredients for the paste in a blender with 2 tablespoons water and blend until smooth. Transfer the paste to a saucepan. Heat and cook, stirring all the time, for 3 minutes. Add the coconut, paprika, hot water, and salt. Continue to simmer, stirring often, until all the water has been absorbed by the coconut, about 2 to 3 minutes.

2 Taste and adjust the seasoning, then add the chives or scallion. Continue stirring over low heat for 2 minutes more.

3 Serve hot, warm, or cold.

SERVES 6-8

PREPARATION
about 15 minutes
COOKING
15-20 minutes

Calories per serving 66
Total fat *7 g (73%)*
Saturated fat *5 g*
Protein *1 g*
Carbohydrate *5 g*
Cholesterol *None*
Vitamins *A, E*
Minerals *Potassium, Iron*

CHILI AND GREEN MANGO RELISH

MAKES ABOUT ¾ CUP

PREPARATION
about 15 minutes
COOKING
about 15 minutes

Calories per tablespoon
27
Total fat *0.1 g (4%)*
Saturated fat *None*
Protein *0.4 g*
Carbohydrate *7 g*
Cholesterol *None*
Vitamins *C*
Minerals *Potassium*

You can use chilies and green mango, cut up as described here, instead of cucumber in the recipe below. Here, however, they are combined with other ingredients and cooked to make something more like a hot sweet-and-sour chutney.

2 tablespoons palm sugar or brown sugar, plus more to taste
3 shallots, very thinly sliced
2 large green chilies, seeded and very thinly sliced
2 small red bird chilies, finely chopped

3 tablespoons rice vinegar
3 small green mangoes, peeled and cut into tiny matchsticks
½ teaspoon salt
3 tablespoons finely chopped cilantro leaves

1 Put the 2 tablespoons of sugar in a saucepan. Heat and stir until the sugar becomes soft and hot, about 2 minutes. Add the shallots and both kinds of chilies. Continue to stir for 2 minutes.

2 Add 4 tablespoons water, the vinegar, mangoes, salt, and cilantro leaves. Stir to mix well. Cover the pan and simmer for 4 minutes. Uncover, increase the heat, and cook, stirring often, until the mangoes are soft and brown and sticky, about 5 to 6 minutes. Taste, and add more salt and sugar if needed.

3 This relish can be served immediately. It will, however, keep in an airtight jar in the refrigerator for about a week. It goes well with most curry dishes and with Stuffed Round Eggplant (page 137).

AJAD
Cucumber Relish

SERVES 4-6

PREPARATION
*about 15 minutes,
plus 1 hour's standing*

Calories per tablespoon
17
Total fat *0.1 g (4%)*
Saturated fat *None*
Protein *0.8 g*
Carbohydrate *5 g*
Cholesterol *None*
Vitamins *A*
Minerals *Potassium*

This is not a hot relish. On the contrary, like the cucumber and yogurt relishes that one finds in parts of India, it is designed to cool the mouth after the hotness of a curry. However, it must contain a small amount of chili. (See page 35)

1 large or 2 small cucumbers
4 tablespoons rice vinegar
2 teaspoons sugar
1 teaspoon salt

1 small red bird chili, chopped
1 shallot, very thinly sliced
2 tablespoons hot water

1 Peel the cucumber(s) and cut in half lengthwise. With a small sharp knife, cut out the seeds from the center and discard them. Slice the cucumber into thin half-moon slices.

2 Mix the rest of the ingredients in a glass bowl, and stir to dissolve the sugar and salt. Add the cucumber, stir everything around, and leave the relish to stand for at least 1 hour before serving.

Cucumber Relish and Chili and Green Mango Relish

HOT EGGPLANT RELISH

In a Thai household, a homemade relish like this is used as a dip for crudités. The family will gather around the low table and eat with their fingers, dipping the cut-up raw vegetables—quarters of small, round eggplant, sticks of cucumber or carrot, or even quartered hard-boiled eggs—in the relish to scoop it up. When using eggs, the relish is usually spooned on each quarter egg, which is then wrapped in a lettuce leaf.

You can, of course, serve this relish just as you would hummus or guacamole, as a party dip.

MAKES 12-16 CANAPÉS

PREPARATION
about 15 minutes
COOKING
*about 15 minutes,
plus cooling*

Calories per serving *7*
Total fat *0.1 g (14%)*
Saturated fat *None*
Protein *0.4 g*
Carbohydrate *1 g*
Cholesterol *None*
Vitamins *A*
Minerals *Potassium*

2 medium-sized purple eggplants, whole
2-4 green or red chilies, seeded and finely chopped
1 shallot, finely chopped
2 garlic cloves, finely chopped
¼ teaspoon salt

1 teaspoon soft brown sugar
1 tablespoon finely chopped cilantro leaves
1 tablespoon nam pla fish sauce
1-2 tablespoons tamarind water or lime juice

1 Half-fill a saucepan with water and bring it to a boil. Put the eggplants in the boiling water. They will float, but they will be cooked in 10 minutes if you cover the saucepan tightly.

2 After about 10 minutes, turn off the heat and uncover the pan, but leave the eggplants to cool in the cooking water.

3 When they are cool enough to handle, take them out and cut each eggplant lengthwise into halves. With a spoon, scoop the flesh out of the skins and put it in a bowl.

4 Mash the scooped-out eggplant flesh well and add the rest of the ingredients. Stir vigorously with a spoon to mix everything well. Adjust the seasoning with more salt or fish sauce and tamarind water or lime juice, and serve as suggested above.

FERMENTED YELLOW BEAN DIP

SERVES 6-10

PREPARATION
about 10 minutes
COOKING
*about 3 minutes,
plus cooling*

Calories per serving *15*
Total fat *0.1 g (5%)*
Saturated fat *None*
Protein *1 g*
Carbohydrate *3 g*
Cholesterol *None*
Vitamins *A*
Minerals *Potassium*

There are two types of fermented yellow beans readily available in Asian markets in the West. You can buy them in cans or jars, either already crushed to a smooth paste (often labelled "yellow bean sauce," see page 22), or with the beans still intact. Here you need to start with a smooth paste, so if you only have the whole beans you will need to blend them first.

8 tablespoons yellow bean paste
1-3 small red bird chilies, finely chopped
2 tablespoons finely chopped scallions

2-inch piece of fresh ginger, finely chopped
1 teaspoon sugar

1 In a small saucepan, mix all the ingredients well. Cook over low heat for 3 minutes, stirring often. Leave the dip to cool. Refrigerate if not using immediately.

2 Serve at room temperature as a dip for crudités, spring rolls, or fried tofu. Any leftovers can be used for cooking Tofu in Yellow Bean Sauce (see page 138).

PICKLED GARLIC

MAKES ABOUT 2½ CUPS

PREPARATION
about 5 minutes
COOKING
*about 15 minutes,
plus cooling and
2 weeks' maturing*

Calories per tablespoon
12
Total fat *None*
Saturated fat *None*
Protein *0.4 g*
Carbohydrate *3 g*
Cholesterol *None*
Minerals *Potassium*

If you don't use pickled garlic very often, you may prefer to buy it ready-made and bottled in your local Asian market. It is, however, very easy to make at home, and I do so regularly. I have a habit of buying long strings of Continental garlic, which sooner or later start to grow green shoots. This is how I preserve them. (See overleaf.)

2½ teaspoons salt
4 tablespoons sugar

6 heads of garlic, separated into cloves and peeled
½ cup rice vinegar

1 Put 1¼ cups of water in a saucepan and bring it to the boil. Add ½ teaspoon each salt and sugar, stirring to dissolve. Then add the peeled garlic. Simmer for 8 minutes. With a slotted spoon, transfer the garlic to a sterile jar.

2 Put the rice vinegar in a saucepan and add the remaining salt and sugar with ½ cup of water. Boil this liquid for 2 minutes, stirring to dissolve the salt and sugar.

3 Pour the liquid into the jar with the garlic. Leave it to get cool before securing the lid of the jar, and store it in the refrigerator for at least 2 weeks before using the pickled garlic.

PICKLED MIXED VEGETABLES

A Thai meal is not always eaten with cooked vegetables or a salad. Freshly pickled vegetables are also popular,
and are often served with a hot rich curry to cool it down a little.

2½ cups rice vinegar
1 teaspoon salt
8 pearl onions, peeled
6 ounces carrots, peeled and cut into short sticks
10 baby corn, cut in halves
1 chayote or zucchini, cut into short sticks
6 ounces broccoli florets

For the paste:
2 shallots, chopped
2 garlic cloves, chopped
1 small dried red chili
2 teaspoons sugar
½ teaspoon salt
2 tablespoons vegetable oil
2 tablespoons lime juice

1 Put the vinegar and salt in a saucepan with ½ cup of water. Bring to a boil and put in the onions. Cook for 2 minutes, then add the carrots and baby corn and simmer for another minute. Add the chayote or zucchini. About 30 seconds later, add the broccoli. Increase the heat and boil the vegetables for just 1 minute more.

2 Transfer the vegetables to a colander, saving 6 tablespoonfuls of the cooking liquid. Refresh the vegetables in a bowl of cold water. Put them back in the colander, discarding the water.

3 Put all the ingredients for the paste in a blender and blend until smooth. Transfer to a wok or large shallow saucepan. Add the 6 tablespoons of reserved cooking liquid. Heat, stir, and simmer for 1 minute. Then add all the vegetables, and continue cooking on a high heat for 3 minutes. Taste, and adjust the seasoning.

4 Transfer everything to a platter and serve hot, warm, or cold.

SERVES 4-6

PREPARATION
about 25 minutes
COOKING
about 10 minutes

Calories per serving *109*
Total fat *4 g (36%)*
Saturated fat *1 g*
Protein *4 g*
Carbohydrate *10 g*
Cholesterol *None*
Vitamins *A, E*
Minerals *Potassium, Iron*

CRISP-FRIED SHALLOTS

Thai people love these as a garnish, particularly on their rice and noodle dishes.

1¼ cups sunflower oil

2 pounds shallots, thinly sliced

1 Heat the oil in a wok or frying pan until very hot but not smoking (about 300°F). Fry the shallots in batches for 3 to 4 minutes each, stirring all the time, until the shallots are crisp and slightly browned.

2 Remove the shallots from the pan with a slotted spoon as they are cooked and drain in a colander lined with paper towels. Leave to cool.

3 When the fried shallots are cool, store in an airtight container in the refrigerator. They will stay crisp for up to a week.

Pickled Garlic (page 147) and Pickled Mixed Vegetables

MAKES ABOUT 2 CUPS

PREPARATION
about 5 minutes
COOKING
about 15 minutes,
plus cooling

Calories per tablespoon *16*
Total fat *1 g (67%)*
Saturated fat *0.1 g*
Protein *0.2 g*
Carbohydrate *1 g*
Cholesterol *None*
Vitamins *E*
Minerals *Potassium*

Desserts & Drinks

In Southeast Asia we generally don't have the tradition of ending a large lunch or a substantial dinner with an elaborate dessert. Climate may have something to do with it, as well as our love of savory, sour, salty main courses. By the time we have eaten all we want of the seafood, the poultry, the rice, and the sauces and vegetable dishes, we are just too full to eat anything more. In any case, whereas it was necessary in the northern parts of the world to invent cooked sweetmeats to round off the meal, we have only to stretch out a hand to pick ripe fruit from the nearest branch (well, almost).

Still—and especially in Thailand—there are desserts, or things that are suitable at dessert time. In the introduction to this book, I pointed out that a traditional Thai menu ends with two dessert dishes, one dry, one with liquid; then comes the fruit. Today, there will very likely be ice cream or a sorbet, so I have included a Mango Sorbet here that takes nothing away from the natural fruit. For the "dry" dessert, there is Sticky Rice and Mango; and somewhere in between there is Mandarin Jelly, made with agar-agar. These are all delicious and healthy ways of ending a meal with the sweetness that most of us crave before bedtime.

At the end of this section I have also included two refreshing drinks made from tropical fruit, which are commonly served to welcome guests and refresh them after their journey.

Tropical Fruit Salad (page 152)

TROPICAL FRUIT SALAD

When you visit the fruit and vegetable markets in Chiang Mai or Bangkok, whether on land or on the river, you will be amazed at the wealth, colors, and variety of the fresh produce assembled before you.

If you are a guest at a party in a Thai household, your hostess will invite you to choose the perfect fruit from a tray loaded with at least eight different varieties of fruit in season. Choose one or two that you fancy, and a member of the family will take them into the kitchen, to come back a few minutes later with a plate of beautifully arranged slices of the fruit of your choice—unadulterated, and with no sugar, sugar syrup, or ice.

I wish I could say the same for all Thai hotels and restaurants. Here, you often need to be wary before tucking into a large bowl of fruit salad, which may have been prepared hours before, its weaknesses disguised by ice and sugar. This is my suggestion for a refreshing fruit salad, to be prepared and assembled no longer than 2 hours before you intend to serve it to your guests. (See previous page.)

SERVES 6-8

PREPARATION
*about 25 minutes,
plus chilling*

Calories per serving *79*
Total fat *0.3 g (4%)*
Saturated fat *None*
Protein *2 g*
Carbohydrate *19 g*
Cholesterol *None*
Vitamins *A, C, Folic Acid*
Minerals *Potassium*

2 ripe mangoes
1 medium-sized pineapple
4 large oranges
1 small golden watermelon or Charentais melon

juice of 1 lime or lemon
5 passion fruit
1 teaspoon superfine sugar (optional)
more halved passion fruit and lime wedges, to serve

1 Peel the mango, pineapple, and 3 of the oranges. Cut the mango into long strips, not too thin—about ¾ inch wide. (Alternatively, the mango can be left unpeeled, cut in pieces and scored as described on page 10.) Cut out the eyes of the pineapple, and cut the pineapple in half lengthwise. Cut out and discard the core, and slice the pineapple into half-moon shapes, also about ¾ inch thick. Slice the oranges or separate into segments, holding them over a bowl to catch any juice; then squeeze the juice from the pith before it is discarded.

2 Wash the melon and dry its skin well. Using a sharp knife, cut it into quarters. The quarters can now be easily peeled if you prefer. Cut each quarter in half lengthwise, and prise out any seeds that you can see to get rid of as many as you can. (If you are using a Charentais melon, all the seeds can be scooped out with a small spoon.)

3 Arrange the fruit on a deep round glass or ceramic platter. Sprinkle the juice of half a lime or lemon over all. Cover with plastic wrap, and keep in a cool place, but not in the refrigerator.

4 Halve 4 of the passion fruit and scoop the juice, including the seeds, into a sieve over a small bowl. With a spoon, press the juice through the sieve, and discard the dry seeds. Add the juice of the remaining half lime or lemon, and the juice of the oranges you saved earlier plus the juice of the extra orange. Finally, halve the remaining passion fruit and scoop out the juice and seeds, adding these to the other juice in the bowl. Stir to mix, taste, and, if the mixture is a little too sour, add 1 teaspoon (not more) of sugar. Mix again. Cover the bowl with plastic wrap, and keep in the refrigerator until needed.

5 Just before you ask your guests to help themselves to the fruit salad, pour the mixed fruit juice over the fruit. Decorate with more halved passion fruit and lime wedges.

MANDARIN JELLY MADE WITH AGAR-AGAR

This is a refreshing sweet dish, typical of Southeast Asia. Agar-agar is a substance extracted from seaweed that will gel even without refrigeration (though chilling makes it set more quickly). In the tropics this is very useful. If you can only find agar-agar granules, these will do—and they simply dissolve in water (follow package instructions). Agar-agar sweets in Thailand are usually made creamy by the addition of a lot of coconut cream and egg; here, however, we adopt a healthier approach, with mandarin and a mixed fruit sauce. You can, of course, vary the fruit as you please.

½ ounce agar-agar strands, soaked in cold water for 1 hour, then drained
1¼ cups mandarin juice (about 6-8 mandarins)
2 tablespoons superfine sugar

For the fruit sauce:
1¾ cups mandarin or orange juice (about 9-12 mandarins or 6 oranges)
2 tablespoons superfine sugar
14-16 ounces assorted fruit (strawberries, sliced mangoes, mandarin segments)

SERVES 6-8

PREPARATION
about 15 minutes, plus 1 hour's soaking
COOKING
about 10 minutes, plus cooling and chilling

Calories per serving *95*
Total fat *0.1 g (1%)*
Saturated fat *None*
Protein *1 g*
Carbohydrate *23 g*
Cholesterol *None*
Vitamins *A, C*
Minerals *Potassium, Iron*

1   Put 3¾ cups of cold water in a saucepan. Add to it the drained agar-agar strands, bring to a boil, and simmer, stirring occasionally, until the agar-agar looks mostly dissolved. Strain the liquid into a bowl, and add the mandarin juice and sugar, stirring vigorously with a wooden spoon.

2   Pour the juice into a flat high-sided plate and chill in the refrigerator.

3   To make the sauce: heat the mandarin or orange juice and sugar in a saucepan until the sugar has dissolved, then bring to a boil. Add the fruit and simmer for 1 minute only. Transfer the sauce with the fruit into a serving bowl and leave it to cool.

4   Take the agar-agar jelly out of the refrigerator and cut it into diamonds or triangles. Arrange on top of the sauce. Serve cold or slightly chilled.

MANGO SORBET

SERVES 6-8

Whenever I can get them, I buy Thai or Manila mangoes specially for this sorbet. These two varieties are very sweet and never fibrous, so they have the best flavor and texture for sorbet making.

PREPARATION
about 25 minutes
COOKING
*about 5 minutes,
plus cooling and
2 hours' freezing and
20 minutes' softening*

Calories per serving *142*
Total fat *0.3 g (2%)*
Saturated fat *None*
Protein *1 g*
Carbohydrate *36 g*
Cholesterol *None*
Vitamins *A, C, E*
Minerals *Potassium, Iron*

**8-10 mangoes, peeled
juice of 1 lime**

scant ½ cup superfine sugar

1 Slice the flesh of the mangoes into a blender. Add the lime juice and ½ cup of water. Blend for a few seconds.

2 Put ¾ cup more water and the sugar into a saucepan. Stir to dissolve the sugar. Bring to a boil, then simmer for 2 minutes. Leave to cool.

3 When the syrup is cool, add it to the mango pulp in the blender, and blend again for a few seconds. Transfer the mixture to an ice-cream maker and churn for 9 to 10 minutes. Transfer the sorbet to a plastic container and freeze for at least 2 hours.

4 If you don't have an ice-cream maker, transfer the mango pulp to a plastic container, freeze it for 1 hour, put it back into a blender, and blend for a few seconds. Return it to the container and freeze again. Repeat this process. Freeze for at least 2 hours.

5 Allow the sorbet to soften for at least 20 minutes in the refrigerator before serving.

STICKY RICE WITH MANGO

SERVES 6-8

People in rice-growing countries do not think it strange to eat rice as a main course and rice again for dessert. In fact, the Thais serve this dish not just as a dessert but as a sweet snack at any time.

PREPARATION
*about 10 minutes,
plus 1 hour's soaking*
COOKING
*25-30 minutes, plus
5 minutes' standing
and cooling*

Calories per serving *186*
Total fat *1 g (4%)*
Saturated fat *None*
Protein *4 g*
Carbohydrate *41 g*
Cholesterol *None*
Vitamins *A, C*
Minerals *Potassium, Iron,
Zinc*

**2 cups of white glutinous rice, soaked in cold water
for 1 hour, then drained
1¼ cups coconut milk
pinch of salt**

**2 tablespoons superfine sugar
4 small or 2 large ripe mangoes, peeled and cubed
mint sprigs, to decorate (optional)**

1 Put the rice, coconut milk, salt, and sugar in a saucepan with 1¼ cups of water. Stir and bring to a boil. Stir again and simmer, uncovered, until all the liquid has been absorbed by the rice, about 8 to 10 minutes. Remove from the heat, cover the pan, and leave it to stand for 5 minutes.

2 Transfer the rice to a steamer or double saucepan, and steam for 15 to 20 minutes.

3 To serve: one method is to mold the warm rice into individual molds or ramekins lined with plastic wrap so that the rice can be unmolded easily when cold. Then, put a portion of unmolded rice in the middle of each dessert plate and arrange the mango around it. Another method is to press or roll the warm rice evenly on a tray lined with plastic wrap, then cut the cooled rice into diamond-shaped pieces. Arrange these on the serving plate, with the mango on top and around. If you like, garnish with mint.

Previous pages left to right: Sticky Rice with Mango, Mango and Jackfruit Drink, Mango Sorbet served with slices of fruit

MANGO AND JACKFRUIT DRINK

This is a very healthy and delicious drink if you make it at home, without sugar, and keep it well chilled in the refrigerator. If you should happen to ask for something which will cheer it up even more, my suggestion would be rum. White or dark rum, both are equally good. Unfortunately, fresh ripe jackfruit is still not easily available in the West, but canned ripe (not green) jackfruit will do very well for the time being. This fruit is bright yellow.

2 very ripe mangoes, peeled and coarsely chopped
1 pound canned jackfruit, drained and well rinsed
in cold water, then chopped
juice of ½ lemon
sparkling mineral water (optional)

1 Put all the chopped fruit and the lemon juice in a blender, and blend until smooth.

2 Add about half a cup of mineral water if you wish. Pour into glasses, and chill until needed.

MAKES 2-4 GLASSES

PREPARATION
about 10 minutes, plus chilling

Calories per serving *160*
Total fat *0.5 g (3%)*
Saturated fat *None*
Protein *1 g*
Carbohydrate *40 g*
Cholesterol *None*
Vitamins *A, C*
Minerals *Potassium, Iron*

MANGO AND PASSION FRUIT DRINK

When the celebrated food writer Jane Grigson came to dinner many years ago, she asked for "your lovely drink." What she meant was one of those delicious fresh tropical fruit drinks which she naturally expected me, as someone from a tropical country, to have ready for guests at all times. I must admit I was puzzled for a moment, and unprepared. After living in England for 25 years, I assumed that drinks before dinner were alcoholic.

2 ripe mangoes, peeled and coarsely chopped
8 ripe passion fruit, halved
1 tablespoon superfine sugar

juice of 1 small lemon
½ cup mineral water

1 Put the mango flesh in a blender or food processor. Scoop out the passion fruit pulp, and sieve it into the blender or food processor. Discard the seeds. Add the sugar, lemon juice and mineral water and blend the whole thing for a few seconds.

2 Transfer the juice to a jug, and chill before serving in stemmed glasses. If you don't have time to chill the juice first, add crushed ice on top of the drink.

SERVES 4-6

PREPARATION
about 20 minutes plus chilling

Calories per serving *46*
Total fat *0.2 g (4%)*
Saturated fat *0.1 g*
Protein *0.9 g*
Carbohydrate *11 g*
Cholesterol *None*
Vitamins *A, C*
Minerals *Potassium, Iron*

INDEX

AUTHOR'S ACKNOWLEDGMENTS

This book is based on half a lifetime of cooking and eating Thai food, and on a number of visits to Thailand. I could not have written it, however, without the help of many people.

For my most recent research trip, Meg Guy of Columbus Communications made a string of reservations for me in hotels of the Four Seasons and Regent Group. I also want to thank Ilona Robinson for giving me many introductions to people with whom she had worked in these hotels.

In Chiang Mai, Simon Hirst, the General Manager of the Regent Resort, and his wife Deborah were my hosts at a dinner of delicious local dishes, and chef David Bedinghaus told me much about northern Thai food. Simon Hirst organized a most useful program of visits to local markets and restaurants as well as to the Royal Project in nearby hills, where my guide was Tanoo Manotham.

In Bangkok, as always, I met my old friends Sombat Bhuapirom and Noot (Mrs Kamolvan Punjasthiti); they answered my questions, and took me shopping in the market and back home with them to cook what we had bought. Also in Bangkok, I want to thank Kurt Wachtveitl, the General Manager of the almost legendary Oriental Hotel, and members of his staff for their interest in my work and their help.

In Australia I must especially thank David Thompson, chef-proprietor of the Darley Street Thai and Sailors' Thai restaurants in Sydney and author of *The Top One Hundred Thai Dishes*, for hospitality and a lot of informal teaching and advice, as well as for permission to use one or two recipes from his book.

Back in London, I am grateful to David Natt for the section on wine for Thai food. I should like to mention Philip Iddison, whose *Thai Food Glossary* has helped me so much. I also want to pay tribute to people who work for or with Frances Lincoln Limited: Jo Christian, the commissioning editor at Frances Lincoln; Lewis Esson, who acted as both Series Editor and Project Editor; Louise Kirby and Anne Fraser; the photographer, James Murphy; and Janet Smith, Kit Chan and Allyson Birch, who prepared the food for James's camera. The general goodwill has been most effectively promoted by my agent, John McLaughlin. My thanks to all of these, and I know they will all understand why I dedicate the book itself to my husband, Roger.

PUBLISHERS' ACKNOWLEDGMENTS

The publishers would like to thank Kit Chan, Allyson Birch and Meg Jansz for their assistance with food styling for the photography and Jon Folland for editorial assistance.

Editor & Project Manager: Lewis Esson
Photography: James Murphy
Styling: Róisín Nield
Food Styling: Janet Smith
Nutritional Analysis: Patricia Bacon
Indexer: Hilary Bird
Page Make-up: Jon Anderson
Production: Jennifer Cohen and Peter Hinton
Commissioning Editor: Jo Christian
Art Editor: Louise Kirby
Picture Editor: Anne Fraser
Editorial Director: Erica Hunningher
Art Director: Caroline Hillier